Nature as Mirror

an Ecology of Body, Mind and Soul

Nature as Mirror

an Ecology of Body, Mind and Soul

Stephanie Sorrell

BOOKS

Winchester, UK
Washington, USA

First published by O-Books, 2011
O Books is an imprint of John Hunt Publishing Ltd., The Bothy, Deershot Lodge, Park Lane, Ropley,
Hants, SO24 0BE, UK
office1@o-books.net
www.o-books.com

For distributor details and how to order please visit the 'Ordering' section on our website.

Text copyright: Stephanie Sorrell 2009

ISBN: 978 1 84694 401 7

A CIP catalogue record for this book is available from the British Library.

Design: Stuart Davies
Cover illustration: Hanne Jahr

Printed in the UK by CPI Antony Rowe
Printed in the USA by Offset Paperback Mfrs, Inc

We operate a distinctive and ethical publishing philosophy in all
areas of its business, from its global network of authors to
production and worldwide distribution.

CONTENTS

I was delighted to be asked to write the Foreword to this book as there are so many aspects to its philosophy that I found intensely inspiring and moving. The concepts that nature does not judge and that, there is nothing wasted in human experience, are ultimately positive and inspirational. This book is also profoundly helpful regarding the eternal problem of mankind's fear of death. Stephanie tells us that death is, in nature, only a steady process of unfolding, shedding and rooting. Nothing and nobody really leaves us because we have integrated their essence within us. Through this trust in nature we are moving towards a philosophy of life that is deeply spiritual. As my teacher, White Eagle, tells us: Do not fear the unknown, not even death itself. For with every forward step you take you are entering a fuller existence. 'Nature as Mirror' helps us to the realisation that through nature, all aspects of spiritual life can be explored.
Jenny Dent, Mother of The White Eagle Lodge, worldwide

Nature as Mirror is a remarkable book which connects the threads which exist amongst all created life. Deep truths are interwoven amongst beautifully illustrated descriptions of the natural world. Perhaps through this book we may actually begin to see who we truly may become.
Jane Sorbi, Mother of the White Eagle Lodge in the Americas

We are finally starting to understand — or perhaps to remember — that we are inseparable from the Earth and that whatever we do to Her we do to ourselves. But it is not enough to know this intellectually. We have to feel that truth in our bones and in our cells. We must learn to live it with every breath. This wise and lovely book can help us do precisely that.

By teaching us to see ourselves and all the patterns of our lives reflected in the natural world around us, Stephanie Sorrell has created a powerful and useful tool for self awareness, spiritual growth and the self-healing of person and planet.
Marian Van Eyk McCain, author of *Elderwoman and The Lilypad List*, Co-Editor of *GreenSpirit Journal* and Editor of *GreenSpirit: Path to a new consciousness.*

An inspiring book which is full of wisdom and activities to guide us through our lives and help us to reach more of our potential. Stephanie uses her own experiences to demonstrate that nature is the teacher and like nature, we can whatever happens to us, regenerate our lives. It is in nature that we can connect with the transpersonal and our spirituality. As a psychotherapist I will find this book invaluable as a tool to use with my clients.

Rosemary Anne Ward, Psychotherapist, MA

Dedication

I would like to dedicate this to my mother who, through her genes and her presence during my childhood, opened my eyes to nature. This is the greatest gift you have ever given me and, as I realize now, was your harbor during your stormy and unsettled life. May the wind in the trees and soft dew of the dawn bring peace to you, wherever you are.

Acknowledgements

Thank you, Hanne, for your belief in my work and your constructive criticism throughout the writing of it. Once more, I am indebted to the loan of your beautiful artwork on the cover.

I am indebted to Jenny Dent for her support in writing the foreword at extremely short notice... and even more, for grasping the meaning, so fluently and well.

To Anne Welsh, who nursed and teased out this 'never-ending' project over the three years I was studying Applied Psychosynthesis.

To My 'sisters' in the Applied, Marguerite Falvey, Heather Jenkins, Chris Roberts and Heather Samson.

To Aubyn Howard and Sandra Visser, for their tremendous enthusiasm and support which sustained me through many a 'Long Wait'.

I am deeply grateful to Chris Brown in Chichester who gave me a safe haven during a year of being homeless.

Finally, I dedicate this to Bosham House where I lived and worked, for its beautiful grounds, where this work was first conceived.

Foreword

The theme of mankind's relationship with nature is an old and beautiful one. Wordsworth in 'Lines Composed a Few Miles above Tintern Abbey' wrote:

'*I have felt... a sense sublime*
Of something far more deeply interfused,
Whose dwelling is the light of setting suns,
And the round ocean and the living air,
And the blue sky, and in the mind of man
A motion and a spirit that impels...
And rolls through all things.'

Yet today the profoundly respectful, symbiotic relationship of man with nature has become for many a frightened retreat from 'natural disasters' coupled with a dawning awareness that our behavior has damaged our natural environment; leaving many of us actively seeking to redefine our relationship with the natural world. It is a conflict between the natural world and the material world that is experienced by everyone, whatever their life situation. In this inspiring book, Stephanie Sorrell helps us to heal our relationship with nature and to use nature's cycles and patterns to heal our lives.

Nature as Mirror blends the ancient wisdom of nature with a very modern, uplifting and readable approach. It is fascinating on more than one level. Firstly, it initiates a way of viewing nature that is healing and moves away from the negativity and guilt found in the modern media. Stephanie is ultimately reassuring, telling us that 'nature will in time regenerate itself' and giving us a positive view of change and progress: a new view of nature is starting to emerge. Now it is up to us to re-evaluate our relationship with the natural world; and the first step is through our inner relationship with nature – which is the second key aspect to this book. Stephanie models a way of living and existing in harmony with nature, a method that moves on from our exploitation of nature by exploring and actively celebrating the power, beauty and wonder of nature; using it as a mirror to our life experiences, forming a vision that guides and sustains us.

The blend of ancient wisdom with modern life is an appealing one. Stephanie invites the reader to work through the changing seasons of their lives, and to use the tree and acorn as patterns for existence. These eternal images are nevertheless fresh, new and relevant to our lives today. In fact this book is particularly relevant to our modern day existence as we are shown how in re-connecting with nature we can heal many of the problems and stresses of our modern lives, such as the constant conflict between 'doing' and 'being'. The book leads the reader in the process of actively 'being' – a skill that so many of us do not possess.

In fact, I feel that this is more than a book; it is a working document, actively inviting the reader to participate in the processes involved. A series of active questions, meditations and creative visualizations lead the reader forward to a place of unique connection with nature and with themselves. I would encourage you to read this book actively – notebook in hand – and do all the processes. Take the leap of actively re-connecting with the natural world and add depth and comfort to your modern life.

I was delighted to be asked to write the 'Foreword' to this book as there are so many aspects to its philosophy that I found intensely inspiring and moving. The concepts that 'nature does not judge' and that 'there is nothing wasted in human experience' are ultimately positive and inspirational. This book is also profoundly helpful regarding the eternal problem of mankind's fear of death. Stephanie tells us that death is, in nature, only a steady process of unfolding, shedding and rooting. Nothing and nobody really leaves us because 'we have integrated their essence within us'. Through this trust in nature we are moving towards a philosophy of life that is deeply spiritual. As my teacher, White Eagle, tells us: 'Do not fear the unknown, not even death itself. For with every forward step you take you are entering a fuller existence.' *Nature as Mirror* helps us to the realisation that through nature, all aspects of spiritual life can be explored.

Jenny Dent, Mother of The White Eagle Lodge

Introduction

Although I started this work in the early 1990s, if I am honest, I began it much earlier. As a child growing up in the 1960s, although money was scarce, I was able to enjoy and value the experience of the natural world around me. Having moved from London to Somerset and then to Essex by the age of five, I was exposed to contrasting landscapes that left a lasting impression on me. My first memory, however, was of wading around in bright red wellington boots in one of the London floods. Water was squelching over the top of my boots and I squealed excitedly as I experienced the current. The Thames had broken its banks and, until the Thames Barrier was completed in 1982 after an eight year long construction project, London was vulnerable to flooding. Actually, the worst flooding occurred in 1953, a few years before I was born and this is when 'Old Father Thames' made a supreme effort to regain its floodplains. Ten thousand people had to be evacuated. But the population has doubled since then, so the dangers of rising water levels due to melting ice floes in Antarctica becomes ever more threatening.

The flooding left a deep and lasting impression on me. In retrospect, it seems incredible that a city as big and powerful as London was built on marshland with a river flowing underneath. But then Venice, world-famous for 150 canals in a shallow lagoon, is also affected by global warming and will have to raise its system of flood barriers to meet this. Then there is New York, frequently flooded by the Hudson River. These, compounded with other low-lying nations such as the Maldives and

Bangladesh, reveals only a little of what is waiting in the wings for us. It is only when the more vulnerable places in the world flood that we realize water fills seven tenths of the global landscape. Living in relative ease on dry land we are apt to forget this. Yet....symptoms abound of increased global warming which expands water and causes it to rise. An ongoing weekly barrage of this trickling through the media makes complacency and comfort less and less attainable. Here, in Great Britain, not only the coastal regions are in danger of flooding, but further inland – in fact anywhere near a river or built on floodplains. On an annual basis it is not an uncommon sight to see swans and ducks sailing down the high street at window level.

In the context of this book, what is this saying, or mirroring on a world level?

In astrology and dream symbolism, water is symbolic of the soul and the emotions. Water is also symbolic of the Great Mother, because of her rulership of the tides as well as women's menstrual cycle.

If water is symbolic of the soul and water levels are rising as global temperatures increase and ice melts, what could this be saying?

Like the waterways we have tried to control by building dams, we have also tried to tamp down the soul. Many of our towns and cities lie on top of natural rivers that have been concreted over. What does this do to the life force of the river which ultimately affects human life? We have built on flood plains and continue to do so in order to make a quick profit. We have drastically changed the earth's natural hydraulic system by endless felling of trees and desecrating the rain forests. The Mayans did this in Central America, and this led to the collapse of their civilization, compounded with overpopulation and bitter wars over dwindling resources. Jared Diamond, scientist and ecologist, believes the downfall of Easter Island with its loss of trees, largely contributed to the nemesis of this ancient civilization, and sees this as a metaphor for what is taking place on a global level at an accelerated rate. In short, trees maintain the water cycles of the planet. Where trees have been razed to the ground, desert settles in their place, after the inevitable floods and erosion of the topsoil. Animals and birds once dependent on the shelter and food trees offer, literally die out.

Yet, unlike our mortal bodies, the soul is indestructible. And now we can no longer ignore the world soul's return to claim back what we have denied her, our own soul life. Water always finds its own level and, given time, erodes its manmade boundaries to reclaim its territory. And in Freudian terms, the unconscious rises up to make its presence known by becoming conscious. No wonder Freud, for all his criticism was sometimes referred to as 'Midwife to the Soul'. As a race we are sick, crazy, out of control so that we have to take our psyche to the counselor, the psychiatrist or psychologist. But our healing can be only as good as the healer, the counselor, the psychiatrist. I have come across therapists, of which there are many, who have seen environmental concern as a projection or displacement of our own repressed desires, rather than a natural response to what has been done to nature.

Thankfully, there are activists and therapists like Joanna Macey and John Seed, who set up a rainforest project in Australia and worked closely with the late Arne Naess, the founder of deep ecology. Joanna Macy has been working since the 1960s to address a collective mourning ritual that allowed participants to work through deeply repressed ecological disaster.

Until we can see that what we do to the earth, we ultimately do to ourselves, we cannot heal. The waters of the soul are rising and wanting to claim us back through our sickness and dis-ease. But the road back to consciousness is not an easy or comfortable journey in contrast with our obsession with quick-fix schemes. Whatever way we look at it, we are in the midst of a global environmental flooding. Our greatest handicap is in experiencing that we have no power; that we can go about our daily life as though nothing is happening. No wonder we keep ourselves busy as a race. Anything to shut out the reality!

I have childhood memories of Taunton with its deep red soil, hills and meadows with leafy lanes embroidered with wild flowers and grassy banks tumbling into crystal clear running water that never stopped day and night. I also remember the red squirrels gallivanting about in areas of parkland.

Clacton-on-Sea returned me to the presence of water in a different way. Until I was twelve and moved again – this time to a boarding school between Oxford and Reading, I grew up with the sea as a living presence in my life. The shrill cry of the gulls was a constant background sound as they squabbled noisily for food scraps. In contrast, the rounded cooing of a pair of stock doves on the chimney was a soothing lullaby.

Whenever I had been away for a week or so, and the familiar salty seaweedy smell would wrap itself around me at the railway station, I would gulp in the air greedily. To this day, I have a tin of shells garnered from my sea visits. I only have to open it and the sea, with its vivid imagery and fresh salty sharpness, rushes up to meet me. At night, amidst rough seas, I would hear the sound of passing ships sounding their fog horns to warn other ships of their presence. My Grandfather would call it 'Mournful Mary' after the wartime siren in Dunkirk.

The sea grew into me, from my introduction at five to my teenage years when I would visit again from boarding school. My troubled teenage thoughts would slow down as I paced the beach. Instead I experienced a deep internal voice that was rhythmic as it was wise and nonjudgmental. As the sea spoke to me, I would prop myself against a boulder or squat on the sands and write poetry. Although I wrote the poetry, it was the sea's rhythmic voice which inscribed itself on the blank screen of my mind and, finally became externalized on a scribbled page of a notebook I was carrying. Over the years many of these poems have been written, some published in gift books worldwide thanks to a publisher who believed in my work. The sea always soothed me and, over time, she became like a maternal presence to me. It was here when I began to compose my first love poems and, as I wrote, I found a way of being with the emotional turmoil that can come with adolescent love and dreams. I learned as the sea could be turbulent and frightening in intensity, she could be calm and still as a mountain lake. As the tide went out, I would find treasures embedded in the sand in the form of shells, seaweed, marbled pebbles or rock pools which harbored a miniscule world of teeming life, I could relate this to myself also. Although the tide of activity and excitement would leave me for a while, it would be an invitation to drop down to a deeper level and find what had been hidden before. I penned these words at Lulworth Cove.

I cannot write this.
The way the salt breeze swoops down from
From white breasted cliffs to tease
The wild grasses.
Or the sea raking the shore below
With her endless white sighs.
No more than I can write the lark
Tumbling harmonies into the endless blue sky.
Instead, I dip my pen into the sea
And write words that vanish unread into coves.
Paragraphs that lie scattered and broken on the sands.
And dreams that are diamond edged as sun strikes water…

Like the sea, my inner tide would turn again and slowly trickle back into those aching hollows, bringing new life and inspiration. In contrast, when the tide rose and rose, so that I felt emotionally and mentally overwhelmed by all the worries of the world and the waves crashed against the rocks, it would become still again and the silence that I loved would become deeper than ever. And it didn't matter where I travelled or lived, the sea spoke all languages and would find me wherever I happened to be.

The sea's voice always found me whether I was living in Brighton, or holidaying on the Isle of Iona, the Isle of Lewis and Harris. It would find me from Lulworth Cove in Dorset, to Yugoslavia and when I lived in Norway for a time on Ulvoya, a small island in the Oslo Fjord. Moving back, when I came to live in West Sussex for seven years, I found it at Bosham harbor where I took my daily walks. It would connect with that place within me that I learned to use and trust as a small child.

Now, as I have made West Cumbria my home for the last six years, in the small town where I live, the tide goes out even further, but despite this always returns. Within walking distance of the village of Haverigg, is Hodbarrow Lagoon, also a wildlife centre for the RSPB. Here, I am able to witness the migrating birds who return again and again to occupy this place during the summer months.

Before coming to live here, my knowledge of birds was rudimentary, confined to breeds indigenous to Britain, such as robin, the various tits, thrushes, blackbird, the finches, several warblers and woodpeckers. Although, when I lived in Chichester, I was fortunate to witness the haunting cries of the peregrine falcons as they made their annual nest in the cathedral spire. Beneath the constant telescope and webcam of the RSPB, I followed the development of the juveniles each year. I marveled then as I often did that bird cries could make themselves known above the clamor of busy city life.

The arrival of the first swallows, swifts and house martins came and I experienced a great sense of relief and joy – they had made it again! Having dared searing heat, wind and thousands of miles to return to this humble place to grace us with their presence. In parts of Africa it was a great privilege and omen of good luck to have a swallow nesting in your house, on your roof.

Sadly, this is rarely so in England where home owners put wire netting over their precious eaves to protect them from droppings. Similarly, I experience a sadness when they line the telephone wires and fences, chattering excitedly, because I know they will soon depart home to a warmer climate, making that heroic passage across the Sahara where many lose their lives.

But as this Cumbrian coastal landscape slowly took hold of me, I began to notice the behavior and breeding habits of the many birds who lodged here .... More than anything, my regular walks around Hodbarrow Lagoon enabled me to get in touch with my creative mind. In the open spaces, of which there are many, my walk round the nature reserve brings me into contact with crested grebes and their fantastic mating display of heads turning in unison and the reed dance where they pull grasses from the riverbed to show each other. The grebe spends twenty percent of its life underwater in its search for small fish and sand eels. Like the swan, they carry their young on their back, small heads peeping through the folded wings. And in watchful hiding, if you look hard enough, the heron waits hunched and motionless; still as a monument in the bulrushes. For me, the heron with its bamboo stilt-like legs, is the epitome of the slow poised movements in Tai Chi; the quiet waiting which, energetically, seems to render the bird invisible. There are the shrill cries of the oystercatchers as they swoop overhead. Spring brings the aerodynamic family of terns; arctic, sandwich, common and little tern who make their passage every year from places as far flung as South Africa and the Arctic. Then there is the eider duck, the adult male with his white and black coloring and magnificent apple-green head in contrast with the dowdy female. I hear their soft 'oo-hoo', like a toned down wolf whistle before I even see them. The prehistoric looking cormorants stand on outcrops of rock in the lagoon, spreading their wings to dry in the wind and sun.

In the six years I have been here, outwardly wrestling against the financial uncertainty that brought me to such an out of the way place, I have been buffeted by outsider's comments as well as the elements. A man who came to deliver goods, cursed the area: 'What you're doing moving up here?' he challenged. 'There's only the prison!' While I struggled with and against settling into the community, these words came back to haunt and mock me. A year into being here, a fellow traveler on the train, a man who had moved up to the area from London, asked as I was getting off, 'How long have you been in exile up here?' Curiously 'refuge' and 'exile' describe the same landscape, but their meanings are far apart.

But, eventually, you do settle in a roundabout way. Things that can't settle or lodge themselves into the barest of precipices finally lose their struggle, and fall off. I found work nearby in Furness General Hospital, working on the nursing bank there, shuttling from medical to surgical level and back again. Reluctant to become permanent, and yet wanting the security it offered at the same time. For those first three years I felt imprisoned in an environment that seemed closed and unfriendly to 'offcomers', the term used for outsiders. I wanted to split and run... but really there was nowhere to run to ... only further north to Scotland, the highlands, then full circle back to Norway. Limited funds forced me to move and kept me where I was, like so many others the world over.

The rise and fall of the tides with its waves reminds me of the rise and fall of sap. The fall, when all the deciduous leaves have left the trees and they stand naked and brittle against the skyline. And then the rising up again in the spring when buds burst into leaf and blossom, and trees experience a new spurt of growth visible in the fresh green needles of the conifers and the concentric lines etched into the tree trunk and limbs. The swelling buds which, later, birth fruit that contains the seeds of the new even as they lie on the ground rotting after the fall, may seed themselves through the beak of a bird or the mouth of a squirrel. This is an incredible insight into the natural world; that even as a life form is dying, rotting away, the seeds of new life are waiting in the wings. We grieve in our belief that life is linear rather than cyclical. In the natural world there are no straight lines, only curves and spirals. That is why the manifestation we witness in the natural world is cyclical, a concept which I work with in the main part of this book.

My mother introduced me to nature because I believe it was her sanity in the midst of her psychotic illness. Despite the difficulties in our tenuous relationship, I will always be grateful to her for passing on that love and awareness of the natural environment. On our walks, she taught me the names of all the wild flowers. She also awakened my love for poetry, its rhythm and ability to evoke the deepest of feelings with such succinct grace. There were poems that she read to me which became deeply engraved across my soul and, although some of them were little known in the shadow of Longfellow, the Rubiyant of Omar Khayyam, Tennyson, Browning, Blake and Wordsworth, they were ones that had been passed down in the family from generation to generation.

My mother grew up on a farm and, perhaps, that was where her love of nature emerged from, but I think it spoke to the brokenness within her, as it did through my ancestral lineage where, sadly, most of the males, my uncle and father included, committed suicide in a final act to escape clinical depression. My mother was an artist and, after her death, I was asked by the estate agent to clear the attic of 'clutter' in preparation for the house going on the market. Up in the attic, I found abandoned paintings piled up against each other in a corner draped with musty cobwebs. One of these salvaged oil paintings hangs in my study now. It is a beech wood and, although the leaves are fiery red and gold, the trees are packed so tightly together that the light never entirely breaks through. But – just here and there, golden light pools onto the reddish woodland floor through impossible openings in the overhead foliage. I remember when I first saw it at sixteen it spoke to me, although I wasn't to understand why until years later. It hung in the room where I stayed, when I visited, for years and then suddenly it was gone, obviously banished to the attic. Dimly, beyond the pooling light is a narrow pathway through the wood and years later I think of the Italian poet, Dante Alighieri. Dante's words in that wonderful rendition of human growth, descent, purgation and spiritual resurrection:

> *In the midway of this our mortal life,*
> *I found me in a gloomy wood, astray*
> *Gone from the path direct: and e'en to tell*
> *It were no easy task, how savage wild*
> *That forest, how robust and rough its growth,*
> *Which to remember only, my dismay*
> *Renews, in bitterness not far from death.*
> *Yet to discourse of what there good befel,*
> *All else will I relate discover'd there.*

I loved that painting because it is literally the only thing I have left from my family heritage. It is the darkness that so many of us endured, but also the light that was salvaged from the darkness. My grandmother's name before she was married into Sorrell was 'Newman' and my mother told me that she was a distant cousin of Cardinal Newman. Although I have never really explored this further, I always smile when I see or hear that hymn of his:

> *LEAD, Kindly Light, amid the encircling gloom*
> *Lead Thou me on!*
> *The night is dark, and I am far from home—*
> *Lead Thou me on!*

Whether Cardinal Newman was some distant relative of ours or not, those well known lines speak so cogently to me. Furthermore, the spiritual thread runs through both lineages of my family, where two of my great grandfathers were priests, one a Methodist, the other Catholic. I still have a rosary that was once my grandfather's and has been handed down through the family. Perhaps I am wanting to say here that spirituality is embedded in nature, as darkness is the shadow that protects us from too much light.

But I think it is more than that. There is something about illness or dis-ease within the soul that turns us away from the world and makes us grateful for all the beauty which emerges from it. I believe suffering whether it is mental, emotional or physical, creates a passage to something deeper, a yearning for a tangible sense of spirituality.

This emerges from many of our children's stories, such as 'The Secret Garden' where the protagonist, brought up in India, finds the key to a secret garden which proves to become the healing salve for both her own bitterness and her cousin's psychological sickness.

I am aware that I may be accused of being anthropocentric by projecting my own unconscious needs onto nature. In this light, there have been many eminent trailblazers along the way in the form of St Francis of Assisi, Thoreau, Aldo Leopold, John Muir and more recently Rachel Carson and Arne Naess. Rather than being selfish or human centered, these pioneers were using the lens of nature to magnify a major deficit in our understanding of nature. They believed that nature did not exist wholly to serve mankind's needs in a form of endless sacrifice, but that we exist to serve each other. Understandably, this viewpoint has clashed with the mechanistic self-serving model of nature as portrayed by Newton and Descartes.

This sixteenth century paradigm uprooted the former paradigm of a world controlled by spirits, demons and magic. The problem was in exiling the ghosts of the past, certain qualities were lost alongside them. One of these qualities was spirituality which brings a sense of purpose and the unknown into the equation. By only measuring what could be directly observed by the five senses, the living world became robbed of depth, vision or spirituality. Proverbs famous words, 'Without a vision the people perish,' stands as true today as it did then. The problem existed in not so much as the dominion and obliteration of the old world paradigm, but in the total exile of anything invisible and spiritual.

In actuality, history has moved forward at an unprecedented rate. Our ability to utilize our cognitive mind to further our understanding of science has precipitated a growing need to not only dominate the earth but interfere with the cycles of nature in the mistaken belief that we can do better. Yet, with every influx of new thought, unless the past is valued rather than wiped out, we swing from one extreme to another. Extremes harbor huge rifts of dissension which, although keep them apart, still work in relationship to each other. Living in a world of opposites we can see that war too often becomes a substitute for solution. Yet, underneath, is the unconscious desire to unite. The relationship between two opposing factions bind them together in time and space. The only quality which will unite them, is a change in consciousness in both parties that can see and unearth the good qualities of the past and invite them into the present. From this change in consciousness, a tenable future can be secured. The rational scientific mind is as important as the imaginative, intuitive mind. The two crave for union so that a third can be born in the form of a new paradigm.

Bringing these insights to bear on this work, we can see this change of consciousness is struggling to unite when a critical mass has been reached. Already, with understanding of the past, we can see today that the old scientific paradigm of objectifying nature has outworn itself. Similarly, the superstitious mind of the western world doesn't find any ground because it has gone from underneath it. So, why can't the past and present unite to give birth to a new paradigm for us to live by? The answer is because our mechanistic way of being exerts a powerful hold on us through our material resources. This power is not merely based on need, but greed.

The natural world is literally becoming consumed by its own outworn model. There exists a deep primeval fear in human consciousness that if we gave up the paradigm of the 16th century, we would become impoverished like the third world countries we are exploiting. The problem is, although on one level we know that we are ultimately impoverishing ourselves by our own greed, we cannot give up our addiction. Greed is an addiction because having more and more and more is never enough. We are on a material helter-skelter, addicted to the 'rush' of an ever greater conquest which will lead to our own demise.

Yet... I do believe that within the matrix of this ageing paradigm of exploiting nature, a new one is endeavoring to emerge. We know we cannot continue to go on in the same way as we have done. The symptoms of planetary degradation are all around us, through the media, through our immediate environment – and, even more, through ourselves. We hate what we are doing, what we are becoming and how we are creating a terrible inheritance for our children and their children's children. The symptoms of the earth have been coming through loud and clear for decades and if we allow ourselves to become unconscious, we will have to stop and take responsibility. Yeats expresses this far better than I in his *Second Coming*.

Turning and turning in the widening gyre
The falcon cannot hear the falconer;
Things fall apart; the centre cannot hold;
Mere anarchy is loosed upon the world,
The blood-dimmed tide is loosed, and everywhere
The ceremony of innocence is drowned;

The best lack all conviction, while the worst
Are full of passionate intensity.
Surely some revelation is at hand;
Surely the Second Coming is at hand.
And what rough beast, its hour come round at last,
Slouches towards Bethlehem to be born?

Nothing is still any more. We cannot stop moving, yet we are not getting anywhere, just running on the spot, eroding the very ground beneath us. And in juxtaposition to this I want to include T.S. Eliot's passage from the Four Quartets

At the still point of the turning world. Neither flesh nor fleshless;
Neither from nor towards; at the still point, there the dance is,
But neither arrest nor movement. And do not call it fixity,
Where past and future are gathered. Neither movement from nor towards,
Neither ascent nor decline. Except for the point, the still point,
There would be no dance,
and there is only the dance.

Chapter 1

Nature as Mirror

When we get out of the glass bottles of our ego,
and when we escape like squirrels turning in the
cages of our personality
and get into the forests again,
we shall shiver with cold and fright
but things will happen to us
so that we don't know ourselves.

Cool unlying life will rush in,
and passion will make our bodies taut with power,
We shall stamp our feet with new power
and old things will fall down,
and we shall laugh, and institutions will
curl up like burnt paper.
D H Lawrence

Psychologists and psychotherapists have long emphasized the importance of authentic mirroring in childhood development. Without this the young human being cannot experience a true sense of self, of his own inner being. Alice Miller writes extensively about this in her seminal work on childhood development; that the child looks at his mother or primary carer and sees himself reflected, and his sense of self is realized and grows. If the parent or primary caretaker has received inadequate mirroring themselves and is unconscious to this, they look at the child and expect to be mirrored and so cannot give the young child what is needed. Such a child, like Narcissus, falls in love with his own reflection and develops essentially narcissistic tendencies which dominate and impair relationship with others. The narcissist fluctuates between grandiosity where he feels all powerful, and extreme, excruciating feelings of inadequacy which leave him depressed and full of shame. By nature he is bipolar with no shades in between. This grandiosity is a protection against an appalling sense of pain and emptiness; a guard against falling into a bottomless trough of shame which belongs to his past.

Briefly, narcissism is founded on the classical story of Narcissus written by the Latin poet, Ovid:

Narcissus was the son of the River God,Cephisus. By the age of sixteen he had grown into a young man whose ravishing beauty appealed to lovers of both sexes. But his pride kept him away from relationship and scorned all lovers. The nymph, Echo fell hopelessly in love with the young man, but was greatly handicapped by her inability to initiate a conversation. Narcissus, growing impatient, rejected her and she withdrew into the forest, wasting away in her grief to a mere voice that could only echo the last few words of everything he said.

The Gods, angry with the way Narcissus had spurned Echo, decided to teach him a lesson by causing him to fall in love with himself. The Goddess who initiated this was named Nemesis, which means retribution. One day, Narcissus caught sight of his reflection in the water and fell in love with his own image. Unable to drag himself away from the hypnotic and dangerous preoccupation with his reflection, Narcissus faded away until he died of starvation.

Since few of us have received perfect mirroring from our parents, most of us if we are honest, possess a certain degree of narcissism in our make-up. But there is a difference between 'healthy narcissism' based on proper self-respect, and unhealthy narcissism with over valuation of the self. Most of us oscillate between cycles of inadequacy and self-satisfaction, but return to the middle ground between. For the narcissist, these polarities are more extreme and there is no middle ground. The strongly narcissistic personality is invariably lonely even if they are the life and soul of every party. Their need to be in the limelight and be special to all never goes away. The narcissist needs to be 'top dog' and, although greatly admired because of this, they are rarely liked because of their total self-absorption and inability to form an equal relationship with others. Because the narcissist's relationship with their inner self is missing, their relationship with others and the world is imperfect as well.

I was fortunate in my training to work with a self-confessed narcissist and felt deeply privileged to learn about narcissism through him as well as recognize my own narcissistic tendencies. Paul was a young magnetic personality who was charming, good looking and could keep a room entertained for hours. Strongly charismatic, he was a natural leader and teacher who dialogued with considerable expertise and eloquence. At first, I was irritated by him because of his powerful persuasive qualities and his need to dominate the room, but gradually as I came to know him and saw the tremendous inner battle he had with his narcissism, his deep vulnerability despite his proficiency in his work, I grew to respect him. He battled with his narcissism daily and although he was totally aware of his compulsiveness, still found it hard to live in his body. Because he had done so much work on himself, he possessed a deep insight into the psychological condition of others; his powers of perceiving the often unconscious intention behind his fellow students and all those under his tutelage and care was unsettling. His ability to sense the 'unspoken' in a room and voice it portrayed a deep and keen sensitivity.

It was, in fact, through Paul that I came to understand my own lack of parental mirroring and the reason why nature had become such a central reservoir of strength, wisdom and comfort in my life as a child.

From an early age I had sought refuge in nature as children often do when there seems no safe place to go or reliable parental figure to turn to. Outside in the country, I felt safe and secure. The emptiness and loneliness I felt inside me drained away in the presence of nature as my fears and anxieties subsided and I observed the world around me. More than anything, I felt nature accepted me as I was. I did not have to *be* anything other than myself. It was through this implicit relationship with nature that a healing began to take place deep in my soul. Although I did not know it, nature had become my mother, teacher and mirror.

The more I looked at nature, the more I saw the journey of my own soul reflected. I saw that nature was inscribed with a life philosophy which was ancient, spoke all languages, was inherently spiritual and close to the heart of all life. It was nature that inspired my sense of poetry which began as a song in me, demanding expression. Writing became the lens through which nature expressed itself.

I saw that in nature nothing is static. Everything is on the move, on the change, in the midst of transformation. From the rock at the bottom of the river which, unseen, is continually shaped and rounded by the currents, to a wider spectrum of alternating seasons, to the bud that comes into blossom on the rosebush. In the midst of the summer, at some point the air changes, becomes sharper and you know within your body that even though you have just passed through the longest heat wave on record, the fall is beginning to stir in the wings and make its presence known. And although, after that the next few days may be humid and summery again, you know there has been a subtle change and the season will never be the same again. Nothing in nature happens suddenly even though when the storm breaks, it may seem so. But as the storm has been building up for days amidst subtle changes in air pressure, the opening of the buds which may appear to burst into blossom one day have been pending for some time. We just have not been aware of the signals. Signals that our ancestors used to read and understand intuitively and the animals know and respond to on an instinctual level. In nature there are no linear processes, just organic ones that oscillate between polarities of fallow and fertility, darkness and light, hot and cold.

As time passed, I came to see that these natural cycles and processes profoundly shape and transform our lives just like the currents shape the rock at the bottom of the river. Nature, like our lives, is not only beautiful and predictable, she is also wild, awesome, terrifying – even cruel. She is not only in the gentle breezes that ruffle the lake's surface and sunlight sending the ripples into coruscating facets of brilliance. She is also the edge of the hurricane, the cyclone that lays waste our feeble attempts to make our mark on the earth. There – burning relentlessly within the implicit beauty of the desert, she is also present within the darkness of wintry days which seem reluctant to let in the light.

Seeing this in nature ironically gave me a sense of security; mainly because I could see that my own internal and external difficulties were not necessarily there because I had *got it wrong*, but because it was an integral part of the process of life. Something always emerged from loss, darkness and sacrifice even if I did not always believe it. The truth of that was inscribed in nature, from the shedding of leaves and fruit in the fall, to the new buds that are there waiting on the frozen branches. As much as I wanted life to be perfect and hunky-dory as depicted in story books, it was a dramatic interplay of tranquility and turbulence with many nuances and shades in between. The problem is, we have created a culture where we have lost all the nuances and shades in between. Things are split into good or bad and within this mindset the glue that holds all things together and makes them pliable is lost. Within this culture of sharp straight lines and mechanized production all the curves and roundness which mark the organic process, have been ironed out. No wonder plutonian forces emerge in our lives without warning and lay waste our belief systems! In exiling the shades in between we have left ourselves wide open to the violent forces which break and reshape us and which we try our best to avoid.

Because nature had become very precious to me, I experienced the relentless destruction of the natural environment keenly. It was as if what we as a race were doing to nature, was being done to me. Although in actuality this is true, because as we destroy and abuse our natural habitat through exploitation of valuable resources, we lessen our chances of continuity as a race. But I personalized everything, attributing feelings to nature that I had not been able to accept in myself. In fact nature was mirroring unconscious painful feelings within me.

Time, like the water shaping the rock at the bottom of the river, lends sense and meaning to things that are too painful to explore at the time. Instead of reacting, I began to become proactive by changing my way of thinking and using visualization to heal the *dis-eased* environment. While I held resentment in my heart for those who were damaging the environment, I was creating an 'us and them' situation which exacerbates all enmity. It also maintains the split between good and bad. I did what I could on a practical mundane level by writing my earth poetry and supporting organizations who worked to bring about global change. Additionally, I came to understand that within me was the destroyer as well as the healer. I could not accept one and reject its shadow. Shadow and light are both valid and integral in nature as exemplified in the candle flame or the shadows that arrive when the sun shines.

This sense of inclusiveness is demonstrated so well in the

story of Julia Butterfly Hill, who in 1997 climbed up into a 1,000 year old Redwood tree that was threatened by Pacific Maxxam logging company. There she stayed for *two years*, and did not come down until a deal had been negotiated with the timber company that they would not clear-cut her tree, Luna, nor the three acres of ancient forest around it. Julia survived in a tarpaulin shelter at two hundred feet above the ground.

This remarkable girl, still in her twenties, wrote: 'The greatest, most positive, and longest lasting change will always come from a shift in consciousness in the heart.' Julia actively demonstrates the power of this when she reveals an incident where the loggers had been clear felling the trees around her with chainsaws for twelve days, where she felt hatred and disgust for them *and* herself that she was part of the same human race. But, with effort, she had to lift herself out of these oppressive thoughts, knowing that her hatred was part of the same violence she was endeavoring to avert. Instead she went deep into her heart, to that place where all life is connected and instead sent out love and acceptance. She describes how the atmosphere between herself and the loggers changed and they began to relate to her as a person rather than an object. Her seemingly small and invisible act had a profound effect. I am reminded of the words of St Francis de Sales, the Roman Catholic bishop of Geneva:

Nothing is as strong as gentleness.
Nothing as gentle as real strength.

Environmental consciousness is a collective dynamic that needs to reach a critical mass for it to change and become fully effective. At the time of writing this we are in the midst of this critical mass which environmental pioneers like Jonathon Porrit, Schumacher, Lovelock, Attenborough have been banging on about for decades. Global consciousness has changed enough to admit we have a crucial problem if we fail to cut back on our use of pesticides and environmental pollutants such as fossil fuels. Although we, as a culture, are far more environmentally aware than we have ever been and are taking critical steps to avert global warming like the introduction of massive recycling schemes and use of wind power, we are still hugely in deficit. Environmental awareness is determined by clinical and scientific observation, so is limited in this way. Until it moves up an octave to embrace the heart as well as the head, it cannot become organic. And until it becomes organic, we are hampered by too much information and statistics to act. That is not to say that we lack the potential to work organically with the environment, but whether we have sufficient time to do so.

Knowing the earth's ability to totally regenerate itself after forest fires, floods and even chemical spills, I have begun to see that nature will in time regenerate itself. And, because whatever we do to nature we ultimately do to ourselves, it is we who forfeit our right to life. As a race, despite our illusion of power and domination, we are essentially vulnerable and powerless in the face of global disaster. Despite all our weapons and sophisticated technological tools we are small and defenseless in the face of the unpredictable, as the Twin Towers disaster portrays. Thousands lose their homes every year through floods as a counter symptom of deforestation. Volcanoes explode, forest fires, hurricanes and cyclones will always be more powerful than us. We do not possess anywhere near the same regenerative resources as nature. In the face of calamity, we all fall down. The greater our illusion of power, the more profoundly we expose our shadow of vulnerability. Overdevelopment on the mental level expressed through technological and scientific expertise, leads to an atrophied capacity to work at the level of the heart. Only the invitation of spirit and soul can lead to balancing of the heart and mind.

If we do not want to forfeit the chances of our life on earth, the most selfish thing we can do is to work organically with the environment in order to ensure our continuity on earth. After all, nature is not out there. We only have to look in the mirror – nature is us.

Working with nature as a healing tool by using the natural environment to mirror the fractures and chasms within the psyche is miraculously taking place with victims of torture today. In 1986 Helen Bamber founded the Medical Foundation for The Care of Victims of Torture and out of this the Natural Growth Project was formed. This inclusion of the natural environment as a healing tool for refugees and victims of torture was initiated by Jenny Grut, a transpersonal psychotherapist. She had noticed through her own frustration with words to describe her own moods, how nature seemed to find them for her through mirroring identical processes within itself. She found that sometimes badly abused victims of torture could reach out to nature in a more relational way than with other people. When expressing the value of working with nature as a psychothera-peutic tool she writes:

'If we do not consider ourselves connected with nature we are in a state of disconnection and this is what shattered lives are about. If we cannot make a link with what is ourselves, we cannot get to know ourselves...'

The Natural Growth Project carries out its work on two allotment sites in Colindale, North London and in Ealing, West London. The clients have a plot each to work on throughout their time there which may range from anything from a few introductory visits to months, even years. Together with the help of the psychotherapists employed there, they work with nature to both uncover and recover their past which they have split off through trauma.

Sonja Linden, while working as writer in residence at the Medical Foundation in 1997, spent a three month stint working alongside Jenny Grut and wrote *The Healing Fields* based on the work going on in the Natural Growth Project. *The Healing Fields* is a remarkable work lending a privileged insight into the lives of the clients at the centre and the moving stories emerging through their work with nature. A psychotherapist friend lent me this book at a point when I was two thirds of the way through *Nature as Mirror* and which came as a confirmation of my lone work with nature over the years together with its importance as a healing tool.

Before we move into the stage of learning how to use the mirror of nature for self-awareness, I want to include a little mythology here whose roots are deeply embedded in time and place.

Chapter 2

Using the Mirror

In the context of this book, nature is our teacher by both her example and way of being. Understandably, there is a lot of unconscious fear towards the natural world because it can take us over and will keep on growing and multiplying long after we have lived our little life on earth. The need to control, prune, and cut down nature has been endemic in our culture since we entered the mechanistic age where machines were used to dominate nature so that its energies and fruits could be harnessed to fuel our hunger for money and power. We now stand at the brink of annihilation as a race unless we change our ways and work with nature and learn to respect her presence here on earth as provider and home maker. We are dependent on nature for our survival on her continuity. Nature is *not* dependent on us. Nature was here before us and will be here long after we have passed away.

Until we can accept that we are not only dependent on the natural environment for our nourishment and continuity, but we are also an integral part of it, we will always fall short of our potential on this planet. The fear of nature and the wild emerges from our refusal to accept our own wild, dynamic beauty. So how do we *be* with nature rather than *doing unto her?*

We learn to look into the mirror and perceive ourselves reflected in nature.

This may start with a walk by the beach and noting the shingles at our feet, whether they are jagged or worn smooth with time. How do we feel as we walk by the sea?

Depending on the sea's mood we will experience an internal dialogue with her.

If she is calm with few wavelets, we may experience a peace within us, or even loneliness, a sense of desolation. Already we have begun to look in the mirror of our being by being aware of the backdrop of thoughts and feelings we experience. Alternatively, the sea might be rough and dynamic, churning the pebbles, slamming against rock and wall, waves crashing onto the beach like the stampede of wild horses. We may feel elevated and excited by this dramatic interplay of sea and wind or, alternatively, feel frightened, overwhelmed by powerful forces we cannot control.

Who can experience anything but awe at the sight of a beautiful sunset or sunrise?

Although there are scientific explanations for the sun shining through dewdrops caught on a spider's web or capturing the droplets of moisture to form a rainbow, the interplay of light, color and form is truly miraculous.

Do we experience joy when the swallows, swifts and geese make their long pilgrimage to our shores? What is it within us that makes us experience sadness when they leave?

Some of us enjoy winter because it awakens our need to hibernate, to withdraw from the outer world and draw strength from our inner world. Others of us, affected by the loss of light, become depressed and ill, only recovering when June comes into being, when the buds have unfolded in a banquet of blossom. Can we celebrate the autumnal fruit or does it speak to something inside us of loss of the light and the deepening that is happening in nature?

Like nature, part of us is visible and conscious, the other part is invisible to us and unconscious. When we witness the falling leaf and fruit, do we wonder what is happening beneath the surface; the descent of the life force in the form of sap to the roots.

Perhaps when we see the rain, we feel low as it reminds of unshed tears within us or on a collective level. Alternatively, we may rejoice after a prolonged period of drought because without the vital ingredient of water our crops will shrivel up and die.

Nature does not judge. It is we who judge and use our analytical mind in a negative way. Parental injunctions, although there to guide and protect the young child, run deep and unless we are aware of them they can become tyrannical rulers rather than helpful guides. Remember, nature does not judge or condemn. But if we heap rubbish onto the environment, there will be a response because we live in a world of cause and effect. Within this matrix resides an invincible law of karma, where we are given the opportunity to right our wrongs. We are standing at this critical juncture now.

The Sacred Hoop

Perhaps, when you walk in nature, you experience a dropping down into a deeper level of being. This does not happen immediately because we live in a world of sensory overload where both visible and invisible conditions are vying for our attention, leaving us fragmented and drained or over stimulated. Because we are used to having to steel ourselves against sensory overload, our body forgets how to relax and become pliable again. This simple exercise while walking in nature, I find calms the body and mind:

Allow yourself to breathe in and out rhythmically and slowly. Just allow this to happen naturally without forcing the process.

Experience the tension in your body, in your neck and shoulders…

Relax your shoulders and as you do so feel your breathing becoming deeper. Do you really need to walk that fast?

As you walk, allow yourself to see and experience your

surroundings.

Can you smell the air? Can you feel the wind or rain, the sun against your cheek?

Know that you have a right to be here now with nature. Nothing is more important than this communion with the natural world.

Accept your thoughts, but let them go as you relax into the landscape.

What do you hear?

What do you see?

You might want to adapt this exercise to suit you as time goes by.

When you see or experience a moment of beauty or insight, write it down on a notepad you carry with you, or remember to drop down into that relaxed space and re-experience your encounter with nature. The act of writing your experience down grounds the insight. That is why if we do not write our dreams down, we forget them and they slide back into the unconscious.

As a child, I experienced the trees and bushes as my guardians and the grass was the body of my natural mother. As an adult, I have experienced this as a dropping down into an older, ancient self that has always been and regards nature as sacred and also my teacher. This happens too when I write poetry which is a song that rises up inside me from the earth and inscribes itself first into my heart and then my mind. It is interesting that the centre in the brain that is responsible for language is also responsible for music. Neuroscience has revealed that music has the power to help patients with language disorders recover some speech. People who have suffered a stroke, have found music instrumental in regaining their speech. I also believe this 'dropping down' happens a lot in the creative experience where the personality takes a backseat and an older wiser part of ourselves translates what we breathe in, what we become inspired by, into a living work. To do this, the mind has to get out of the way or surrender to a higher collective mind that is not handicapped by the personality. Sometimes, however, the personality, when awed and unafraid by the inspiration, remains conscious, allows itself to be imbued and changed by the inspiration. But, too often, the personality rushes in to claim what they have been imbued with, as theirs! And the creative work becomes undermined by the personality and may not be fully expressed until the persona becomes 'dead' or silenced.

I do believe the wisdom of the Native Americans lives on because their personalities were servants to their inspiration rather than the other way around. Humility is the opposite of pride and this comes from knowing that we are no better or worse than anyone else. We are all the same: Wakan Tanka's children in the great Stream of life. That is why works thrive so well after people have died because that is when they really come into their power. I am reminded here of a story entitled *The Light*, included in a book *God Loves Laughter* by William Sears.

Once upon a time there was a little boy. With all his family and friends he was lost in the valley of darkness. Then, quite by accident, he found a flashlight. When he switched on the light of the torch everybody in the dark valley saw it and came hurrying towards it. With his light, the little boy began to lead the people out of the valley of darkness and up the path of the mountainside. First a hundred followed him, then a thousand, then tens of thousands. Every time he looked back there were more people behind him. The more people he saw, the more pleased he became with himself and the fine work he was doing. He kept looking back more frequently to see how many he was leading out of the darkness. How proud he was that so many people were following him. But then he stumbled and dropped the torch which was scooped up by someone behind him. The crowd tramped over him and left him in the dust as they swept up the hill. They had not been following him at all. It was the light they were following, and without it he was left in the darkness.

Because the journey of nature through the seasons is circular, we are invited to deepen our vision each annual seasonal cycle. For me, no body of people understood the power of cycles better than the American Indian whose teaching is embedded so much in nature that there is no 'us and them' relationship, but 'I' and 'Thou' as defined by Martin Buber in his seminal work about the power of relationship. To the North American Indian, all life is sacred. In this context, the birds (winged ones) animals (four footed ones) the fish (the finned ones) and the human (the two footed) were not divided by levels of higher and lower, because they were enmeshed in the same fabric of life. When the white man came to North America, his divisive and blinkered ways were unknown to the peace loving Indian who lived in harmony with all life and understood that Wakan Tanka, the Great Spirit, infused all sentient beings. The Indian listened to nature and found his strength in that. In comparison, the white man arrived disillusioned with his way of life where leaders did not act as servants for the people as in the Native American tradition, but abused their power instead. Because they had long lost sight of any sense of justice and the Christian God they worshipped was a punishing and unfeeling God, their view of life was already corrupted. When they found the New World, they wanted it for themselves and looked upon the Native American as backward and inferior because of the way they dressed and the simple way they behaved. Really, the true nature of spiritual and ethical impoverishment was the other way round. It was the White Man who had lost sight of the threads that bind all living creatures together in mutual trust and resorted to senseless acts of violence.

Black Elk was a medicine man of the Lakota Sioux. The Lakota were originally referred to as the Dakota when they lived by the great lakes, however, because of European settlement, they were pushed away from the great lakes region As a sick child, Black Elk experienced a series of visionary experiences and dreams which were to become a trustworthy template for his work as a shaman. He spent the rest of his life struggling to carry out the work and meaning that was embedded in these early visions. Like so many shamans and indeed holy people, such as St Teresa of Avilia who suffered grave physical illness, this was the wound through which the spirit entered and called them forth to engage with. True shamanism calls the healer through his wounding, not necessarily the other way round.

It is Black Elk's words which I use here which underline the importance of circles in the turning of the seasons:

You have noticed that everything an Indian does is in a circle, and that it is because the Power of the World always works in circles, and everything tries to be round. In the old days when we were a strong and happy people, all our power came from the Sacred Hoop of the Nation, and so long as the hoop was unbroken the people flourished. The flowering tree was the living center of the hoop, and the circle of the four quarters nourished it. The east gave peace and light, the center gave warmth, the west gave rain and the north with its cold and mighty wind gave strength and endurance. This knowledge came to us from the outer world with our religion. Everything the Power of the World does is done in a circle. The sky is round and I have heard that the earth is round like a ball and so are the stars.
The wind in its great power whirls. Birds make their nests in circles, for theirs is the same religion as ours. The moon does the same, and both are round.
Even the seasons form a great circle in their changing and always come back to where they were. The life of a man is a circle from childhood to childhood and so it is in everything where power moves. Our tipis were round like the nests of birds and these were always in a circle; the nation's hoop – a nest of many nests where the Great Spirit meant for us to hatch our children.

We can apply this on a broader level to nature whose rivers

are naturally curled and serpentine, unlike our man-made dams which are straight and work against the natural harmony of life. Climbing plants grow in a spiral, winding themselves round and around their training rod or host in a clock-wise direction.

It is popular today in groups that are centered around spirituality, psychotherapy and psychological healing to form a circle. In a circle, everyone is equal and is an integral part of the group. Groups that are modeled on the old way with a speaker/teacher/authoritarian at the front, facing out and the audience facing in, empower the speaker. Energetically, this feels very different. In the old fashioned model where the speaker is empowered the 'audience' becomes disempowered and, because of this, regress to a childlike state. Maybe you can think of examples of this in your own life and how each model impacts on you energetically.

In the next chapter we look at the tree and its journey through the seasons as a working model and template for this book.

Tree Blessing

May you be like a tree whose roots quarry deep
Into the earth's wisdom,
so that your mind is filled with vision and inspiration.
May you grow strong like a tree knowing your growth,
however slow and painful, is not just for yourself.
but for this lovely planet.
May you pause like the tree to feel the gentle winds of
heaven upon you,
and the heart of the Creator warm and golden within you.
May you be wise as the tree who taps the centre of its
being for truth,
so that amidst every storm that shakes your roots
you will know that all is well.
Within your still centre may you know the magic
of love that opens all doors and heals all pain.
May you always be strong and firm and beautiful as a tree.

Stephanie Sorrell

Chapter 3

The Tree as Model

Goethe, the eighteenth century poet and philosopher, believed there were two great lines of evolution. These are the animal and plant. According to him, the culmination of the animal line of evolution is the human being. Similarly, the tree is the end product of the plant line of evolution. I believe, instinctively, we know this to be true. Why else would trees have played such a prominent role throughout history, both mythologically and spiritually? For example, Yggdrasil is the Nordic World Tree and in the biblical Garden of Eden we find the Tree of Knowledge and the Tree of Life.

For many, trees are the spiritual guardians of this planet and since they represent the physical lungs of the earth, this holds true. What I love so much about the tree is that its progression through the seasons illustrates our own inner processes so well. And although its branches extend outwards and upwards to the crown, its trunk stands firm because its roots are embedded so deeply in the earth. Similarly, a true mystic is one who has their feet planted firmly on the ground in order to translate the wisdom accessed into one that is palatable to others.

It is interesting to note on a purely practical level that chlorophyll, the green-yellow product that makes photosynthesis possible, is remarkably similar to human blood. They are both made up of four basic elements, oxygen, carbon, nitrogen and hydrogen and in chlorophyll, the fifth is magnesium. In blood, the fifth element is iron. It is this last and fifth element which makes leaves and plant life green. Geneticist and environmentalist, Suzuki and Grady write, 'The one significant difference in the two structural formulas is: the hub of every hemoglobin is one atom of iron, while in chlorophyll it is one atom of magnesium....... Chlorophyll is green blood. It is designed to capture light; blood is designed to capture oxygen. I find this remarkable and this led me to research further for my own interest.

There is an internet site that gives more information on this including where liquid chlorophyll is ingested orally instead of blood. People who have suffered blood loss through physical trauma or prolonged anemia have seen their blood count go up significantly after taking chlorophyll. Magnesium itself is used for anemia and bone conditions particularly during the female menopause. This should be taken in conjunction with calcium as this helps the body to absorb magnesium. There is a lot of interesting evidence that supports this. Wheatgrass contains 70% chlorophyll and alfalfa is high too. Obviously, this is very important for Jehovah's witnesses whose religion does not allow them to accept blood transfusions.

Returning to the two great lines of evolution cited by Goethe, I believe as human beings who have reached the culmination of our evolution, we have a lot to learn from the tree as representative of the plant kingdom. This learning experience needs to be harnessed through opening our minds and hearts in receptivity to the plant kingdom rather than through the dominance we have exerted in the past. The trees, although not as physically agile as we are, have the advantage of not being dependent on us in the way we are dependent on them, not just for valuable resources, but simply for the air we breathe.

As a child, I was surrounded by trees. My grandfather was a retired farmer and had an orchard which I spent a lot of time exploring and playing in. I loved the rough craggy bark of the old Beauty of Bath apple trees. There was a plum tree with wide open boughs which were made for sitting in; a cherry tree with shiny rose stippled bark that became a profusion of white blossom each spring so that it looked as if a wedding had taken place. There were pear and damson trees, a mountain ash tree which the birds pillaged the berries from each winter. And then there was the magnificent laburnum whose dark varnished branches would send out long cascades of lemon icicles each spring.

My grandfather had given me a plot of land under the orchard to grow my flowers. Flowers that I salvaged from the compost heap and coaxed back to life and marigolds that I grew from horseshoe shaped seeds that resembled cat's claws. My borders were made of shells gathered from visits to the nearby beach with my bucket and spade. As an only child I passed a lot of hours sitting up in the branches of these trees and I believe this is when I developed my early relationship with them and they rooted themselves within my soul.

Enid Blyton's *Faraway Tree* introduced me to an inner and exciting world of trees through her stories. *The Faraway Tree* series focuses on a magical tree inhabited by a motley bunch of fascinating characters. The tree has access to a series of worlds that appear without much warning at the crown of the tree. The world changes each time the young schoolchildren protagonists climb the tree and enter this magical shape shifting space. Some worlds are friendly, others challenging, exciting, even frightening.

Despite her much maligned literary shortfalls expressed by adults too learned to appreciate the lens of the imagination, Blyton's books were immensely popular with children. This dear old writer, whether she knew it or not, was introducing a primitive form of shamanism into her work. Basically, the shaman through a combination of ritual, will and medicinal herbs, enters an altered state of consciousness and climbs the 'world tree' to find medicine for a patient or the tribe. Within the locus of the upper world, the shaman encounters strange and wonderful beings who bring insight into his patient's condition. Although, as everyone knows, shamanism has ancient roots that predate Enid Blyton's work by hundreds, thousands of years, she was inviting the child's pliable mind to explore these ancient roots.

Even though the worldly part of me confessed that *The Faraway Tree* was fictional, another, perhaps wiser part of me insisted that the concept of it was true. Always, even now, I look up into the branches of a tree and remember the story and wonder. Through my passion and love for trees I explored the mythology of the tree and found it to play a central part in all world creation stories. Linking this historical material with the botanical knowledge I had at ground level, I conceived a model I could work with. The model was using the tree as a mirror for our own inner and outer processes.

Models of Consciousness

Besides the cyclical processes of birth, death and regeneration through the seasonal passage of life which is demonstrated throughout this book, the tree itself becomes a complete map of consciousness itself. Much later, when I studied the Kabbalah, I discovered that the kabbalists perceive the 'tree of life' which is central to the Kabbalah, as a model of consciousness too. For them, this map of consciousness extends into four levels or worlds which, in turn, are accessed through a multitude of pathways. This model of consciousness is comprised of four worlds: the spiritual, creative, emotional/intellectual and the physical world.

The founder of psychosynthesis psychology, an Italian psychiatrist by the name of Roberto Assagioli, produced the egg diagram in 1965. This has been used extensively since as a model of consciousness. He divides the egg up into the lower unconscious, (1) middle unconscious (2) and higher unconscious (3). In the centre of the middle unconscious is a small field of personal consciousness (4) and will, called the 'I' (5) where we tend to live out our daily life. At the apex of the egg resides what he termed the 'Self' (6), a centre for higher 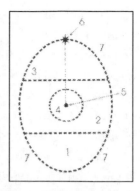 consciousness and will. Outside the egg lies the collective unconscious(7). Through working with our personal stories and history which we may have relegated to the lower unconscious and where our fears, complexes and ego drives reside, we can clear the way to make contact with the Self. This may be experienced by being less 'driven' in a compulsive way to think and act out unconscious behavior, releasing the capacity to make choices which are free of parental, cultural and historical injunctions. The 'I' which is the vehicle of Self may, through understanding of its personality issues, find itself increasingly able to be in dialogue with the Self so that the personal will is in harmony with transcendent Will. Alternatively, work with the higher unconscious through prayer and meditation may cast light on more unconscious processes driving the personality, or it may find this too painful and split off from the lower unconscious so that what is seeking to become conscious and transformed is driven underground and repressed instead. This can be quite dangerous because what is not accepted within the self is projected outwards onto others and the environment. Additionally, the repressed ego can masquerade as the Self in order to be included and there may be all sorts of conflation issues between upper and lower levels of consciousness, precipitating identifiable symptoms such as delusions of grandeur, feeling special, feeling chosen etc. This too is demonstrated in the study of the Kabbalah where, primarily students who wanted to be initiated into the Kabbalistic teachings, would not be allowed to do so until they were at least 40 years old and well established in the world, either through family and children or a career. Even today, in Jewish mysticism students are encouraged to balance their studying with daily mundane activities in the world which reiterates the importance of grounding.

I have found my tree model fits in very well with Assagioli's egg diagram. Here, the upper branches correspond with the higher consciousness, and the fitly named 'crown' becomes the point where contact with super consciousness can be made. The 'I' which symbolizes the part of us that relates to the world is moveable, up and down the axon of the tree. As it takes up position with whatever it identifies with; from middle everyday consciousness to the upper world and lower world. The roots of the tree are embedded in the lower strata of consciousness, that which we are basically unaware of. As Assagioli demonstrated in his work, the lower and higher unconscious are not independent of each other, they are inter-related. What happens on one level, affects the other level. In fact, it is through the identification with one level of being and the exclusion of the other which causes a split between upper and lower. Those who are spiritually polarized, denying material on the ground level, become unbalanced by their denial of lower less palatable ingredients of their make-up, the compost of life which feeds and sustains our roots. To compensate for this imbalance, the ego becomes inflated by feelings of being special and self-importance. Jung referred to this as the 'shadow.' Within the polarity where identification is only made with the mundane everyday world and where there is a persistent exorcism of the upper consciousness, the incarnated self feels that something is hugely missing and may compensate by acquiring a wealth of possessions to fill the hole. The life becomes spiritually impoverished which has profound repercussions on all levels.

Whatever the polarity, there needs to be a breakthrough in

awareness which brings insight into realizing that what we are running away from and avoiding is what we really *need* to sustain us. Childhood, adolescent and cultural experience will determine our polarity. Flower-power generation parents often birth children that are very grounded and immersed in the material world as they learn from the mistakes/imbalances their parents made.

Many of us who have undergone sustained periods of meditation or been away on a retreat may find that, shortly after what seemed like a transcendental experience, there is a sharp jolt back down to ground level. This may even manifest in the form of a sudden illness, an accident, debt or loss of job. Although this is hard to understand, it is a natural way of the system struggling for balance and equilibrium. Work on the upper level will always evoke work that needs to be carried out on the ground level and vice versa. Long subjugated memories and anxieties may surface, even though we felt we had laid these to rest a long time ago.

Similarly, after a long period of trudging through difficulties on the ground level which may be experienced as a period of depression or loss of faith, direction and purpose will precipitate a breakthrough on the upper level. The light will suddenly appear and bring insight and healing to the situation in a most remarkable way. That is why it is important to 'stick with it' when the going gets really tough and irksome. At the point of greatest suffering, a breakthrough is about to emerge. It's rather like the egg timer where time in the form of sand runs through an hourglass and when it has run out, the egg is done. In order to get the sand to flow again, the egg timer has to be turned upside down and the cycle begins again. The sharp jolt from one polarity to another is like being turned upside down literally

As there is no waste in nature, there is nothing wasted in human experience, even though our culture has a huge deficit in dealing with waste with long historical patterns of burying waste rather than recycling it like our third world neighbors. Although now, as a culture, we have begun to work in terms of recycling on an outer level, we can begin to apply this same principle to our own life by looking at the tree again.

In the fall, the discarded leaves form natural compost and minerals which sustain not only the biosphere of the tree but the greater biosphere. What no longer serves on one level automatically serves on another level. Likewise, when experience no longer serves us and we change to embrace greater experience rather than turn our backs on the past, we can utilize this valuable experience as compost and fertilizer in the form of wisdom. A wisdom which can form the foundation for subsequent generations to build on. For example, if it had not been for Bill Wilson's alcoholism, Alcoholics Anonymous (AA) would never have formed. This is true for the multitude of self-help groups which are available today. What no longer serves on one level, serves on another by serving the 'greater good'. This is the true expression of real service, and service is a natural process. Ironically, it is all the things that we want to revile in ourselves that gives us richness of soul and vision which cannot be bought or traded, but lived.

One of the reasons I have chosen the tree as a model for the natural process is because it is something we can see and understand and also mirrors a continual self-replicating process within ourselves. In nature there are no straight lines; river and streams follow and create natural curves in the landscape. The deciduous tree is a mini ecosphere which moves through a cycle of seasons. We can see the seasons engraving themselves in circles upon the cross section of a trunk. The tree's cycle of seasons are held in these widening circles. The elements that have formed its character through buffeting winds and frozen winters, lend each tree its unique individuality. In the tree is an ever unfolding cycle of continuity which begins with the rising sap in the spring and its descent in the fall.

The Seasons

The seasons become a living map through which we process and retrieve our life experience. These seasons are cyclical and ongoing, giving us countless opportunities to explore more deeply into the process which underpins all life, all works of art and gives breadth and depth to the creative process.

Each spring we undergo a *Rebirth,* a return to the beginning of a fresh cycle with all its challenges and opportunities. We are given the opportunity to not only learn from our past failings, but to actually rewrite and recreate our own script. As we move into late spring, early summer, we enter the *Blossoming* part of the cycle. This is the 'in love' stage whether this be towards a person or a creative work of art. We have been impregnated by an idea, a child of some kind and we can experience this as a honeymoon or become apprehensive of what we feel is expected of us. This is when we can really shine. Yet, how many of us want to shine with the heavy expectations placed on us?

As the blossom falls away we can see the swelling fruit beneath. We are entering the process of *Ripening.* As what we are pregnant with swells, we can look forward to a new life, a unique way of manifesting in the world, or we can become very afraid of the impossible expectations we are placing upon ourselves and be tempted to abort our 'baby'. Late summer, early fall finds the fruit we have birthed ready to harvest. This is the time of celebration and 'give away'. We learn about the challenge of giving up what we most love. Our children are not ours to keep. They have their own journey to make into the world.

In the fall, we enter the *Stripping* period where the things we thought belonged to us are taken from us. We learn that we own nothing. Everything is transitory. On a lower octave this can be experienced as a period of grieving, mourning for what we feel we have lost. On a higher octave, we can experience relief, a sense of being unburdened by the trappings of the world.

As fall gives way to winter, we enter *the Long Wait,* which marks a period of seeming cessation of activity. This is divided into, 'known waiting,' 'transformative waiting' and 'waiting in hope'. This period of cessation in activity may seem endless when each day seems the same and there is no evidence of anything waiting in the wings of our life.

Finally, towards the late winter, early spring, we enter the *Wilderness* which marks an extended period of whittling and eroding of the ideas, thoughts and objects which we used to identify ourselves with. Within this period our sense of isolation is deep and long because this marks a dark night of the senses as illustrated by St John of the Cross in his 'dark night of the soul.' Yet, if we surrender to this process, we can enrich our lives with deeper meaning by understanding the quality of being rather than the endless treadmill of 'doing'. We surrender to grace and enter into our own wisdom by the process of *reflection, contemplation* and *aspiration.* And then the great cycle begins again. These cycles can cover a period of beginning and completion in our lives. They do not have to work in correspondence with the seasons of nature, but because they are seasons of the soul, they duplicate the same process. These seasonal passages creates a map and mirror for us to see our inner process reflected. We may be in the midst of several cycles at once. By seeing our lives and inner development in correspondence with nature we can begin to understand where we are in our cyclical process and experience a sense of inner rightness. Our challenging experiences in life is often not a result of what we are doing wrong, but what we are actually doing right!

Death Anxiety
One of the greatest unspoken fears of the human condition is 'non being' and death anxiety. Existential psychotherapists will say that most of our defenses are an effort to block or mitigate these feelings. When they break through into our sleep state, we call them nightmares and we wake up in the night sweating and

full of terror. So great are these fears that many are driven to drinking themselves into a state of near anesthesia or escaping through illicit drugs or prescribed drugs.

Psychotherapist, Dr Irving Yalom devotes his latest book to this, *Staring at the Sun, Overcoming the Dread of Death*. The interesting thing is that when asking one of his clients what she feared most about death, it was not death itself she feared. It was the fear of all that she *hadn't* done in her life! The life she hadn't lived. His client was a successful therapist who, together with her husband, made a lot of money between them. But despite her lack of financial worries and apparent success, there was a large part of her that was unlived. Her drawers were stuffed full of drawings and paintings she had never finished. She had started out as an artist and had received a lot of accolade around this in her early days, but then she had worried that she could not make enough money from it, even though she and her husband had more money than they needed.

This 'unlived' life is what keeps most of us running around frenziedly in pursuit of constant activity like hamsters on tread wheels. And I am thinking of the words of one of my tutors in psychosynthesis: 'We betray ourselves by our security needs.'

Irvin Yalom believes this betrayal of ourselves is the root cause of our death anxiety. If we cannot live the life we came here to do, how can we die with dignity and peace?

The unlived life has a powerful hold on us, because we have forsaken our genetic program and lived the program of our society instead. Yalom goes on to suggest that we may harbor this betrayal of self in a covert way by telling ourselves that we could have lived our life that way if we *wanted* , but we *chose* not too. What a comfort to know that we could have been successful and fulfilled our destiny if we had really wanted to. But what a betrayal also!

This is precisely why our society is the way it is; why we are unfulfilled and even if we are materially successful why we cannot take comfort from this?

Because we are part of an organic process that is ongoing, life gives us countless opportunities to birth our unlived life. These invitations are cyclical much like the template of the tree. After a long protracted arid period in our life where we feel emotionally and spiritually impoverished (*see Wilderness*), spring makes its presence known; inviting us to return to base and begin again. The tree is a template for our process. And if we are very much in tune with nature, we will find that our own process is in harmony with nature as in seasonal affective disorder where there is often a need to hibernate and sleep.

And within this template there is no such thing as death, only a steady unfolding, shedding and rooting process. From the *Long Wait*, the aridity of winter, new life is waiting underneath to push through in the form of buds. If you look carefully at a tree, these buds exist in juxtaposition with the leaf that is getting ready to fall. The fallen leaves return to the ground, forming a mulch, a compost in which insect life, worms and a myriad of other creatures feed from. And now that the leaves have fallen, the waiting buds can slowly swell into ripeness which, in turn, open into blossom, before ripening into the fruit ready for the harvest. What has not been harvested falls and becomes food for wildlife, birds, squirrels, hedgehogs, foxes, late bees and wasps.

What is left becomes compost for the earth and the seeds themselves lie in the earth waiting for their time to come. Each year the cycle begins again, part of a continuous process from bud to harvest and leaf fall. Death does not enter into the equation because it is all part of a continuous process. Similarly, we can see this ongoing cycle repeated in anything from mountain ash, to acorn to chestnut and walnut trees.

In the first part of this work I have used the acorn from the oak tree as a working template as it is something we can more easily relate to. We can hold it in our hands, study it, and watch it grow. Furthermore, it is both 'seed' and fruit. In contrast, the seeds of most conifer trees are small like pine kernels and easily lost. Redwood seeds are even smaller, like fluff which is incredible since they are the world's tallest trees.

In the main body of the book I refer to the apple tree as a model. This is because all of us, the world over are able to relate to this tree. The Greeks were growing apple trees 300 years B.C. European settlers brought apple seeds and trees to the New World and records of apple trees growing here date back to the 16th century. Also, the apple appears in the Christian creation myth of Adam and Eve. It was in actuality the Tree of Knowledge.

As we shall see from the next chapter, Birth of the Light, the acorn has everything it needs within it to be a mighty oak tree as the egg holds the unborn image of the young fledgling or human baby.

The miraculous truth about birth is that the seed, the embryo, the egg contains everything it needs to become itself. Within each lies the genetic code to become a living functioning being. But the life process begins as soon as the seed, egg and embryo interact with their environment. As the acorn draws sustenance from the soil, it grows and slowly emerges. The fact that we come into the world with everything we need to become fully what we are, often becomes lost or forgotten in our obsession with the world around us, our need to have possessions or be like other people, rather than ourselves.

Chapter 4

Birth of the Light

In the beginning was the light. Within this light was all wisdom,
knowledge and life. This was all the acorn needed to know; that
everything it needed to sustain its existence was within it...
And around it...

The light within the acorn wanted to grow, and it was important
that it remembered these things for soon it would begin a very
long and arduous journey that would take it to the depths, but
also to the heights.

The acorn's journey is our journey. The beginning is the life
and awareness of individuality within a greater all pervading
consciousness. Once this awareness of individuality dawns,
along with the sense of separation and isolation it brings, a
yearning to unify with that greater consciousness is realized. The
life force within the acorn or within the self aspires to that greater
consciousness, to the sun and to the light. This aspiration is like
a single ray that pierces the darkness of the soil, the unconscious,
and makes contact with the outer or greater light. Inner light
aspires to outer light and a sense of completion is felt. The initial
sense of isolation and separation is replaced by a sense of
belonging and home. It is reminiscent of the proverbial story of
The Prodigal Son, where the long lost child has reunited with its
parent. And this in a sense is true, for it is the contact and

awareness of this parent consciousness which will urge the soul on in its growth and development. This is in Kahil Gibran's words; 'the breaking of the shell that encloses our under-standing.' It is also the birth of the light within us.

Because we can become so caught up in our journey, it is easy to forget the acorn's simple truth; that everything we need to sustain our existence is within us, or that we carry the light within us. We become distracted so we believe that what is *inside* us waiting to be tapped is *outside* us. We lose touch with our centre of being, or our hearts and become cut off from our roots which are our source of nourishment. We become restless in our search for that part of us which we have denied. It is as if we become like cut flowers in a vase, living an ephemeral existence as we move from inner and outer location, forever gazing through the windows of a prison of our own making.

Here, I find that affirming the following simple truth brings me back into alignment with my centre and source: 'We are spiritual beings having an *earthly* experience. We are not earthly beings seeking a *spiritual* experience, as we may confuse ourselves into believing. We are the light manifesting through matter.

The distractions are many; and that is the life pattern of the spiritual warrior, to be distracted; to be deflected from our quest. The great dichotomy is that when we forget the acorn's simple truth: that everything we need is within us, we start amassing things that we do not need towards us. And this is not to say we should not have material things because we are after all, living in matter, but we become *attached* to these things. Attachment creates a co-dependent relationship between us and the object or person that we are attached too. Our energy goes to the person, object or situation rather than to our growth. But as no experience is ever wasted and is fully utilized on its own merit, these attachments are valid. We still grow, but we grow distortions. We develop galls and growths like a diseased tree. This becomes individual development and soul experience which is more often than not, quite painful. It is interesting that, scientifically, galls are believed to be the evolutionary predecessors to the first fruits. From another perspective, we can understand that these attachments can later give rise to fruit when we move beyond this experience into a greater awareness. From the pain of these attachments and the suffering it evokes in the soul, blooms a wisdom that is unique because it is *ours*. Wisdom is always a living experience, whereas invariably knowledge is second hand and is only animated by the personality of the individuals who are able to inject it with their own life force. I am reminded here of the great American mythologist, Joseph Campbell, whose lecture halls were always overcrowded because he could empower the ancient cultural myths with his wisdom and set them in motion in everyday life. In his time he not only awoke the long slumbering archetypes of the past but created a new mythology to live by.

As most of us well know, life provides us with innumerable opportunities to let go of these attachments. Like the tree, we pass through a cyclical period of shedding, both of leave, fruit and branches. We literally become dead to various conditions whether these are relationships, careers, homes or long cherished dreams. This too is painful, yet through this process we become closer to the light inside us. Stripped and naked, divested of all the grandeur of the ego, we are more receptive to the inner light. This is certainly true on a physical level where our eyes are not only more sensitive to the light after being in a darkened room, but also after a long period of illness where ordinary daylight can be so blinding that we have to shade our eyes. With less distractions mentally and emotionally, we become aware of what is essential and important. We also become aware of how little we really need as there is a dawning awareness of how much inner treasure we have. Living close to the light, we become happier and more fulfilled even though we have less. We live more purposefully and see that the outer world is like a crazed animal that cannot rest. And in turn the world looks at us and regards us as a crank, a weirdo; because if it were to accept and synthesize the ideals we represent, it would be too materially threatening.

Yet as time passes and the scorn that kept us sane gives way to compassion, the World recognizes our light. We become like magnets. People are drawn to the light within us and we in turn surrender to this light, allowing it to shine through us. We enter into our 'soulhood'. We become like the mature tree spreading our branches to give shade and shelter and offering our fruits to those who want them. We have returned to our source and we have not so much lost our individuality as had our individuality transmuted us onto a higher octave. The light within us has transformed us.

But there is a lot of fear around individuality and enlight-enment. As much as many of us want to become enlightened beings we, quite understandably, resist becoming part of an amorphous mass without freedom and the expression of free will. It is our individual consciousness that keeps us in a state of isolation. Yet, if we were to recall the moments of real joy in our life, they are usually born from the realisation that we are not alone, that we are part of something else, whether it be a group of people, nature or when we feel truly inspired to create or produce something. Inspiration occurs when we allow the life force or greater consciousness to breathe through us, to fill us. When we experience happiness in others, we say that they are radiant. The light is shining through them. Radiance embraces, reaches out. A person who has this radiance we refer to as charis-matic.

So we are able to perceive that rather than being isolating, joy seeks to unify. It is the ego that fears its own loss, dissolution and separation because this is what we give up to unify. The light within us dissolves separation because it is its nature to do so.

It could be interesting to take a little time out and reflect on some of these points.

Can you remember when you felt inspired?
What was going on in your life then?
Did you do anything creative with the inspiration?
Did it cause you to feel more sure of your life direction?
Can you go back to a time when you really felt part of something greater than yourself?
Allow yourself to relax into this experience.
What are the feelings going on inside you? Where were you?
Did this experience happen in nature, on a retreat or with a partner?
What has this experience given you?
Stay with this sense of unity and becoming for a while.
If you have not experienced that sense of unity, do you know why? Have you not allowed yourself to feel part of something else?

In the next section we will look at how we suffer the breaking of the light, of becoming spiritually aware beings. How the deepening of the light awakens us to our own innate divinity but also to that within all life. This is a process that engages us on the spiritual pathway with all its insights, breakthroughs and areas of individual and collective transformation. The birthing of the light can give rise to intense feelings of inner loneliness and alien-ation from our fellow man. As we will see, these feelings are natural and symptomatic of any awakening process.

The Birthing Process

Although rebirth can happen many times throughout our lifetime in the form of spring which is cyclical, the birth of the light happens only once and may be long and drawn out or sudden and unexpected. Once the light of awareness dawns there is no going back to the old way of life. It is that light within us which leads us onto our own unique path to realize it more fully.

It cannot, will not give up on us, even if we choose to give up on it. It is a path that may take us through great fear, obstacles, humbling us in many ways, yet it is one that imbues us with a strength and wisdom that the mundane world cannot give us.

The light emerges into our awareness at the point where the secular life can no longer satisfy us. It manifests at the point of our greatest pain when we are brought to our knees and cannot go on any more in the way we have been doing. We can no longer fight and resist. We can only surrender.

There are events and situations in our life that are dynamic enough to completely shatter the foundations of our belief system. This may be precipitated by a death or a loss so deep that it leaves us stranded in an alien world. This is very much the *Wilderness* experience (see chapter 11), a time when everything we held familiar is stripped away and we find ourselves like a stranger in a strange world. We feel so cut off from our environment that it is as if we are in exile. Even our friends have become strangers, and our personal environment appears to be pushing us out. We no longer belong where we used to be.

And yet nothing seems to stand in place of the old and fragmented life. Although every door seems to be barred against us, no new doors have opened. Amidst all this isolation and desperation we have to *trust* and *wait*. Acknowledging our utter powerlessness and breakdown of the ego, we have to surrender to the force that will eventually empower us. Although the mind and emotions may feel tried and tested to the limit, on another level we are actually experiencing the opening of the *heart*.

It is important to remember that this is not the time to reach out. And by this I do not mean denying the help that may be at hand, as long as this is the right kind of help. In fact any attempt to reach out while in this process may throw us back against ourselves. As any attempt to distract ourselves in the world may be either rejected or plunge us into a greater sense of alienation.

We need to keep in mind that because our old life is passing away, simultaneously something new is struggling to emerge: new life as miraculous and unexpected in every way as the chrysalis emerging from its cocoon. And again we have to picture the acorn in the earth, vulnerable and unborn – but despite this, with all the potential for life when the right conditions occur.

This is the time for consolidating energy rather than expending it from already exhausted supplies. We need to draw inward; sit with the apparent inactivity and inner blindness and trust the process. Remember, everything that we need is *within* us. And if we feel we are suffocating in our own darkness, it is important to remember that light is the other side of darkness. The greater the period of darkness, the greater the light that will emerge from this experience.

Nothing in the world will give us what we need and this sense of alienation from the environment we thought we knew is an important step in our process. Unable to communicate in the language of the world, we drop down deeper into a state of receptive being. Within this quiescent sentient state of our being is a soul language. If we internalize our listening and attention we will hear it. It will tell us that we are in the right place, and to trust what is happening or apparently not happening inside us. In fact there is no such state as inactivity. Something is always going on inside us even if we are not aware of it. And we can no more remain in this blind state for ever than we can remain in the sunlight for ever. All events pass away and metamorphose into a different state. On the great wheel of life, all inner and outer manifestation is part of a cyclical process.

This withdrawal from the secular life gives energy to our inner process, which is one of consolidating the inner light. Within this *tomb* of inactivity and darkness, we are nurturing a *womb* of light. As time goes by we feel the pressure of the light within. A useful analogy of this would be a night storage heater which gathers energy during the night and lets it out during the day.

The pressure that we feel, is the pressure preceding any birth experience. It may be uncomfortable, painful even frightening if we do not fully understand what it is. There is nothing we can do to resist it because this power and energy which is pushing through, is so much greater than ourselves. The more we resist, the greater the pressure, and the more explosive the break-through.

Emotionally, as this pressure builds, we may swing between polarities of excitement to a deep and crippling sense of fear. This is natural, for we are facing the unknown. And however many times we undergo birth experiences, each birth is unique and affects us in a different way.

The contractions have begun. We have made a commitment inside ourselves to give birth and the conditions are right.

The acorn is about to split open.

Creative Visualization Exercise

Breathe slowly and deeply and with each breath feel a letting go of the distractions of the outer worldly mind; the frustrations and pains. Instead, feel yourself entering a warm safe place; you may visualize this in the form of a cave or even a shell. Within this place is an altar with a light burning on it and maybe there is a figure here, a maternal figure who welcomes you like a long lost child and loves you unconditionally. Here, you do not have to feel shamed by the inadequacies you feel you have. She can see beyond your outer manifestation to the perfection that is within you. Here there is no judgment, only acceptance.

Meditate on the light and slowly breathe it into your body, first through the crown of the head, then feel it trickling like liquid through your lungs, your heart, arteries and veins of your body, arms and legs, right down to your fingers and toes. See your whole being pulsating with this light. Lastly, concentrate on your heart area, and breathe a soft rosy light into this place until you feel your heart opening like a beautiful rose to bathe in soft pastel rays.

When you feel peaceful and the time is right, leave the cave and gradually breathe yourself back into your body. Know that you can return to this place of healing often and that it is inside you for as long as you need it to be.

This daily contact with the light will help strengthen your inner light and bring you more fully in touch with the process.

In the next section we explore the rooting process in our life through the template of the acorn. How easy is it to feel rooted in our spiritual tradition as well as in the world? We look at some of the issues that prevent our ideas taking root and coming into form. We also look at the creative process and what may be behind our fear to make a commitment to matter.

The Acorn's Journey

The acorn felt the pressure of what was inside pushing against what held it there. As the shell of the acorn cracked, the life inside it broke through the constriction and began to grow, first the shoot reaching upwards to the light, then the roots pushing down into invisibility. This first shoot strengthened with each moment; for the continuity of life and expansion depended on it. The acorn had begun its great journey towards becoming more fully what it was.

The journey begins the moment life commits itself to matter. Within this great fusion enough energy is released to give birth. The shoot emerges from the acorn and, drawn to the light, propels itself to the surface of the soil. This birth is a twofold process, first the shoot that awakens the acorn to the light, then the roots that plunge down into the earth. Once the shoot has emerged into the light, the roots push down into the earth. A commitment has been made into matter and form. Ironically, the rooting process is so vital and crucial to the future development of the organism that it is hidden from visibility. This initial birthing process into matter happens within us too. First the seed kernel is born and embeds itself deep in the unconscious until the light of consciousness draws it up to the light and into manifestation. Then as the seed kernel becomes birthed in matter, the rooting process follows. We can say that this twofold birth process is an idea whose time has come.

Although this initial rooting process happens only once in our own life as in the tree's, the analogy repeats itself innumerable times throughout our own growth and development. This is richly illustrated throughout our language when we 'allow things to take root' and we get to the 'root of a problem.' In fact this process takes place each time we embark on a new venture, whether it be a relationship, career or creative project. Because the rooting process is so vital, it is important that we understand what is going on underneath the surface. Rooting takes *time* and *patience*. These are two qualities which the material world does not esteem very highly; where emphasis is put on instant growth and visible production and nature is 'hurried' along to match this need. The rooting process cannot be hurried. There are no short cuts. If the process is skirted around, then we jeopardize the very foundation on which we are planning to build. Trees that are not rooted deeply or extensively enough, are the first to fall. We know from experience that if we try to hurry a relationship or a creative process, it does not have sufficient time to develop, it flounders.

Let us look at the creative process more fully.

Before an idea can assume shape and form, it is subject to an inner process which takes place within our unconscious. This is where it germinates within the medium of the intangible, unknowable and darkness. It is interesting that most inspiration will come at night in the still quietness of the intuitive world. Since most of us are blind to what is going on in our unconscious and dream life, we may be totally unaware of this process. Those of us who are more in tune with our internal cycles, may realize that something is going on because we feel uncomfortable, blocked or even restless. Because all our energy is held in the unconscious, little headway can be made in the world, hence the blocked feeling. The temptation at this stage is to become frustrated with this state of 'rooting and just being' and unintentionally abort the process so that we are left with an even greater sense of emptiness and lack of fulfillment. How many creative projects are aborted in the early vital stages of rooting because we become impatient and admit; 'Nothing seems to be happening!' The great paradox is that when nothing seems to be happening, an awful lot is going on underneath the surface!

Here the tree contains an essential truth which accentuates the importance of the rooting process. The extent of the root span is approximately equal to the spread of branches and in some cases, even to the height of the tree. In actual fact, the more time and energy that is given to this unconscious process, the greater the potential for diversity, stability and outward expression for our idea. If we want a productive creation or healthy relationship, then all the underground spadework is essential.

From my own experience, I have discovered that if I went through an extended illness, depression or a rigorous test that involved a lot of hard work and assimilation, it was all preparation for another 'branch' to emerge in my life; one that would be beneficial to me and yield a lot of valuable fruit. And, in retrospect, I have always found this to be the case. This really makes complete sense when, in wanting to develop a new career or a change of expression, we have to go through an extended learning and assimilation period which will qualify us for our new position. It is so important that we allow ourselves enough time and energy to prepare for this; that we root it all. A doctor or surgeon who has the responsibility of looking after people's physical health, will need a lengthy rooting/ training process. This allows them to specialize. In less obvious cases we might use an alcoholic like Bill Wilson as an example. His lifelong struggle to give up drinking which, although seemingly very destructive, actually provided the groundwork for the start of Alcoholics Anonymous. Now today, this highly successful organization has yielded thousands of 'branches' all over the world. The fruit that has come as a result of that one man's mission, has had far reaching results into the illness where, often, science and medicine have failed. An interesting point here is that Bill Wilson believed in a power greater than himself, and this principle still stands today. He recognized that very few alcoholics, many of whom came from difficult family backgrounds, could accept the idea of God and religion, so he referred to it as a 'Higher Power', concentrating on the spiritual aspect rather than a religious one. His physical roots were actually set in a spiritual foundation. This is pure alchemy; the transmutation of the base will of the ego to the spiritual or divine will.

Likewise, if we are undergoing a difficult situation; one in which we cannot see a way through, maybe it's worth remembering that this is all part of the rooting process which will shape our future. Unless our inner vision is sufficiently developed, it is not always possible to perceive what is going on underground in order to understand what is happening. Although, with experience, our vision begins to adjust.

For the tree, the soil is its source of food and water. It is from these vital minerals, the rich humus, which derive from broken down animal, insect and plant tissue, that the tree finds its sustenance. Basically its sustenance from the earth is created from the waste products of matter.

Similarly, our source of inner food is developed from the breakdown of earthly or worldly experience. These experiences may have chafed, embittered and tested us to the limit of our endurance. And because of this, either through denial, coupled with the need to 'get on' with the rest of our life, we have relegated it to the unconscious. But however awesome and difficult these experiences may be, they are, nevertheless, fodder for soul making. Our soul has chosen to incarnate here in order to have these experiences, so that it can synthesize them into the wisdom that will help it on its journey. The bedrock of all root growth comes from waste products; because waste products are rich in nourishment. In this way it serves the new developing growth as the fertilizer and manure on the fields aid the development of the young crop.

It is a great temptation to separate the earthly worldly life from the spirit, but this is like separating the mother from the father. They are two complimentary roles working together in the process. This is demonstrated in the wisdom of many of our ancient cultures who believe that the earth is the mother and the sun and sky the father.

Although there is one major tap root which, if damaged in the transplanting process, can endanger the survival of the tree, the root system of a tree can be complex according to the type of tree and soil conditions in which it grows. Trees that grow in areas where there is little water and where the soil quality is poor, will drive their tap root down deep and their roots will extend outwards near the surface as well so they can make use of as much moisture as possible. The fact that a mature tree can lose several hundred gallons of water in moisture through its leaves daily, puts the great necessity for roots into the right perspective.

In juxtaposition, the rooting process within the fabric of our life prepares for the future if it is to survive. We know on a mundane level that although our income may sustain us from week to week, we need to have a cache put by to tide us through sudden unexpected expenses. On a spiritual level this is important too. We might be able to cope with our daily life when things are ticking over smoothly and it is easy to be lulled into a false sense of security, hypnotized by the monotony of everyday events. But when a sudden trauma, like a death or accident confronts us, we encounter our edges and that is when we need to draw on hidden resources. Building up this source of spiritual supply on a daily basis through meditation or contact with nature, or whatever makes us feel at peace, gradually accumulates within our soul. It is important to be like squirrels and make provisions for lean times with the bounty nature bestows upon us. Abundance is cyclical and occurs relatively little when there are long periods without any type of sustenance.

Yet.... ideally and paradoxically we should also live in a state of trust where our needs are met. I do know people who live like this and to a certain extent I have had to learn to live like this myself when I have received several crash courses on how to do this in my life. But material trust cannot be based on the material alone. Trust has to develop from the accumulation of spiritual wisdom we have gained. Alternatively, ultimate trust is more of a state of surrendering and unlearning rather than something we have to develop. We are all born with it naturally and we can see this sense of trust in most small children, but we forget how to trust when we put our faith in the material world and in people rather than the inner life. Inner and outer life compliments each other. The more we put our faith in the material world, the more it lets us down. It is like setting our foundations on quicksand. Yet the material world becomes friendly and works with us if we have our foundations in the spiritual life. Spiritual abundance attracts abundance on all levels, if we by then still want it!

Our sense of rootedness will change throughout life. Young people may positively resist putting down roots, wanting to explore many areas first and this is quite natural. Alternatively, they may be desperate to become rooted and settle down. There is nothing particularly wrong with this either. Our varied personalities, life experiences and backgrounds will make us want to move into particular areas. For most of my life, I rebelled against the so called conventional way of settling down. People used to ask me; 'When are you going to tie yourself down?' Those very words fell like a life sentence on my ears.

I lived with my husband ten years before I married him. Although we were together sixteen years, it was only after we had split up that I have been able to feel more 'rooted' in myself and in the world. Ours was a very co-dependent relationship based on a mutual emotional insecurity. We depended so much on each other that we grew as one root. Before coming together we had not had the opportunity, like so many people, to connect with our own individual needs. On our own we were birds with a single wing that could only fly together. Through standing within my own terrifying sense of vulnerability I have learned to trust my other wing to grow and become firmly rooted in my own truth.

Having explored the acorn, together with its awakening to the light and rooting process, we are ready to move onto the main section of the book: The tree and its cycles from *Rebirth* to the *Long Wait*. But before we move onto the next phase, there is an exercise here which may enable you to see where you are in the section we have explored, what is strong in us and where we may need to develop.

Before we move onto the next phase, take time out to connect with your sense of rootedness. You might need to close your eyes to get in touch with these aspects, or write them down or express yourself in drawing.

What conditions in your life make you feel rooted?
Which people make you feel rooted?
What do you need to do to feel more rooted?
Does being rooted frighten you? If so, is this because you don't feel ready for it?
Can you experience the difference between being rooted materially and rooted spiritually?
Do you feel balanced in these areas?
Where does your security lie?

In the next part of the book, we look at the actual cycles of the tree and how they translate into our own life, growth and development. These cycles, as in the natural world, play out on a regular basis. By exploring each part of the process we can find wherever we are in our own process reflected. With the advent of spring emerge fears of being visible, and the need to shine, to be more fully ourselves.

Chapter 5

Spring: Rebirth

Yes, of course it hurts when buds are breaking
Why else would the spring time falter?
Karin Boye

For a long time we have lived, breathed and seemingly died during the winter period or the *Long Wait (see Chapter10)*. We have almost become creatures of our unconscious – caught up in a world of dreams and symbols that have become increasingly more real and tangible to us. So much dissolution has taken place within and about us. Dissolution of dreams, beliefs and ideals. In fact, we have almost abandoned the thought of returning to the demanding life of the secular world again. But...

New life is stirring within. More, it is pulsing with energy which fills us with a sense of excitement. Yet – still we feel vulnerable and naked. We need more time, but...

There is a sense of urgency — new unexplored avenues await us, and our vision is returning... But, this feeling is so much stronger than us.

Unlike the underground experience of the initial birth of the light, the rooting process, the sort of rebirth that the spring offers, always manifests on a conscious level. It is nearly always visible in the form of a newborn child, or a job, a change of career direction, a new friendship or relationship, or even a move to another country.

Yet, before we become swept along in the celebration of new potential, acquisition and direction, there is always the tremendous fear, conflict and resistance before birth. Sometimes we forget this while we are caught up in the anticipatory events of the future and then wonder why shortly before the event, the birth, we want to run away, abandon the whole thing or terminate the project! It is important to remind ourselves that it is perfectly *natural* to experience these crippling fears; for it is quite literally the final death throes of the old before the new can emerge. As the Swedish poet, Karin Boye, writes about the bud which is about to break, whether it feels pain, we have to remember that although birth is painful, the tearing away of living flesh like the piercing of the virgin's hymen, is ultimately overshadowed by the new and the difficulties of the past are carried away by the waiting new life. An example of this is after the long exhausting labor when the mother sees her baby for the first time, she forgets all about her grueling ordeal and radiates happiness. The pain and discomfort are totally eclipsed by the joy of birth.

This is not to belittle the labor of giving birth. In fact, like all cycles, the end and beginning of each one is crucial and dangerous. Many of us *do* abort the process just before manifestation. Buds do fall from trees, from flowers, from roses and will never open. Although this is sad in that we have stuck with the process yet, at the final hour, abandoned it, it is important to look at it philosophically. Birth or rebirth comes again — and again. It is cyclical. When and if we are ready, we will see it through. Life is just as much about experience as giving birth.

All this brings to mind a journey I was about to make across the Himalayas in 1992. This was the first time I was making such a long journey by myself. Although I was travelling with a guided party, I had never met any of my fellow travelers that I would be in close proximity with over several weeks. I also had a fear of heights – but I loved mountains! Caught up in the excitement of it initially, I was rather taken aback when a lady came up to me and said: 'Don't be surprised if you have second thoughts about going nearer the time or a lot of fear coming up.' She smiled reassuringly. 'It's perfectly natural.'

Nearer to the time, I was grateful for her warning. Up came my vertigo, my dislike of walking on icy surfaces and innumerable others fears and inadequacies that I did not know I had. There was nothing wrong with the decision I was making, it was the old fearful part of me that needed acknowledgement. The part of me that prefers to remain in its comfortable risk free rut. I will always be grateful to that lady, because she gave me permission to have fears. It was okay to be afraid. Just knowing that was therapeutic in itself. Next time, try giving yourself permission to be afraid and see how differently you feel. Being afraid does not mean lacking courage. Courage is being afraid and doing it anyway.

One of the reasons why we feel afraid before we give birth to anything, is that we don't trust ourselves. We do not trust this new untried aspect of ourselves to have everything it needs to fulfill its potential. If we can look upon the *Long Wait* and the *Wilderness* (see chapter 11) as a crucible in which some aspects of ourselves are dissolved and other parts of us created, we can perhaps come to grips with this alchemical process taking place within us. We are not the same as we were. We are changed. We have made space to receive a new influx of energy which is transformative. That energy is already within us, already magnetizing everything that it needs towards it. No two springs are alike. The tree is not the same every year. It has grown, filled out, lost some branches and gained new ones. It has grown in order to accommodate its new self. The same law applies to the cyclical process of the seasons each year, but each spring the form will be different. It will have expanded in new ways; its underground root system will have deepened and spread out. *Whatever is emerging has all that it needs to carry it through to the next stage.*

Basically, spring is a period of expansion, breakthrough, productivity and energy directed into that which is new. It is growth into a whole new area which, although it might happen quite by chance, we have usually been wanting or waiting for quite some time. It brings with it new hope, renewed strength and the need to be cared for. It demands our energy, even *all* our energy; for it is life in the making and we cannot fail to become absorbed or lost in its expression. There is also the sense of working towards an end – a goal. We want to see the project through to maturity. After all, we have a responsibility towards what we have given birth to. It is also a learning experience as all growth processes are. Although we may feel a great sense of duty and responsibility towards our children, it is important that in our efforts to guide, we do not close our senses to what they have to teach us. There is always a symbiotic relationship on an educational level as well as physical and emotional level between parent and child. For example, our new job, even though we may not like everything about it, has a lot to teach us about ourselves — and also in preparation for our greater maturity. Children often teach us as much as we can teach them, and even more. Their lives lie closer to the Great Unknown than our own. They have emerged from there through us. In contrast, we have done our best to forget and avoid the Great Unknown. That is why we are so lacking in trust. Our children awaken us to what we have forgotten, our true purpose. They reawaken our heart, our soul even though we might have tried to build a wall round them in an effort to fit into the world or avoid becoming hurt. That is why children frustrate us and cause us more pain than anything else. They too often represent all that we have locked away, closed down to or denied within ourselves. But it is also why they open us up to joy, vulnerability, beauty, spontaneity, simplicity and so on. Because when we deny what is vulnerable and sensitive within our own lives, we deny

69

ourselves the joy, beauty and peace they can give us. What we give birth to is for our greater growth and development. What we give birth to can remake and reshape our lives — if we allow it. Spring is a miracle! Rebirth is a miracle!

Listening and receptivity are the ears of the soul and the means by which we assimilate information and learn. Despite the frenetic activity that the birth demands of us, it is important we stand still and listen to what arises within us, or we may be in danger of missing the whole message of the experience. Although lessons are repeated until they are learned, it is much more comfortable learning through the senses of the soul rather than through the physical and emotional senses which may be traumatized in an effort to make us stop and listen. Accidents *never* happen by chance. That is a myth. They often occur as a last resort, a wake-up call to our soul to listen, to take note when everything else has been exhausted. If we do not listen or see the warning signs, then the alarm sounds.

As long as we are here on this planet, participating in the vast theatre of life, whether it be in relative obscurity or through the lens of publicity, we *will* give birth. We are never too old to give birth in the realm of the soul. Our purpose here is to learn and to give birth to what is inside us.

Birth might be daunting and frightening but it is also energizing and exciting; for it is pure and unadulterated life force. If you feel blocked, stagnant, then set about giving birth to something, even if you do not know what it is. Get in a position of conception by being receptive. Inevitably, birth will come.

Our attitude towards spring, together with the sort of feelings it evokes, will give powerful clues to how we feel about the birth process within us.

How do you feel when spring comes?

Do you feel excited? Relieved? Exuberant or energized? Does it fill you with hope? Or perhaps you experience apprehension, anxiety and even fear – as if everything is happening too fast and outside your control?

Remember, all these feelings are valid, even though we, perhaps, feel they should not be. Of course we should feel joyful to see the spring after the cold grey days of endless rain, the stark landscape and the unrelenting dark skies. Failure to experience this joy may make us feel guilty and full of despair. After all, it is acceptable to feel low and depressed in winter and during the fall where a lot of people suffer from SAD, but feeling down in spring is different.

Yet contrary to this public belief that spring is wonderful and which society seems to inflict on us, there are many people who find spring difficult and winter infinitely preferable. There are more suicides in spring than any other time of the year. Never underestimate the power and strength of new life and, remember,everything has its polar opposite which is a time of letting go, death, if you like, in the fall.

I once had a colleague who always suffered from crippling depression each spring. Analyzing it, she found it was because she felt she could not keep up with the tremendous outpouring of activity in nature. She would become full of expectations she could not possibly achieve, and this touched into her own feelings about giving birth to her own child; how she felt unable to cope. Once she realized this and gave herself permission to feel the way she did, the depression eased.

Right and wrong, what is acceptable and unacceptable are so often mandatory creeds dictated by society which, in turn, are created from a mixture of material, religious and parental fears and expectations. Our own experience is right for us at the time. It is ours. All we have to do is own and accept it, and ultimately try to understand it.

Basically, in giving birth, the self is moving out of the restriction of the womb that has nurtured it and moving into a greater freedom. It is death and life, death to the old, life to the new. We have outgrown ourselves.

After the meditation we will move onto the next stage in the tree's cycle, the blossoming and see how this impacts on our life.

Meditation

Slowly, withdraw your energy from the outer world by using your breathing to calm your body and mind. Take time to do this. Experience yourself as a pure stream of consciousness.

Become aware of your own tree, using your sense of smell as well as your vision. Notice that it is stippled with firm buds along the stem and branches. You are drawn to one bud in particular and as you gaze at it, the bud becomes bigger and you find yourself inside it..... You become aware of the ambience of spring green around you and the soft silk of tightly folded leaves. As you open your senses to the experience so that you find yourself enfolded in the soft newness of it all, you become aware of a growing pressure within you. Yet there is a pressure outside; a growing warmth and light that invites you out, to extend your boundaries.

Take a few moments to explore the tension of this; the rightness of your immediate environment. The excitement of the light which is getting brighter and that you feel is urging you out. Be aware of the push- me/pull- me dynamic of your state of being.

Be aware of the conflicting feelings within you: the need to burst out of you environment that seems no longer protective but imprisoning. But, also the fear of breaking out into an area that you have never experienced. An area full of light, waiting to greet you, and yet the fear of leaving the womb of your safe haven that has been yours for so long.

The pressure reaches an optimum point where there is no going back and yet...

You long to return to the safety of being enclosed.

You can hear voices now, inviting you out.

A soft fragrance impinges on your senses and then you release a cry as that which kept you imprisoned for so long gives way and you find you are in blossom. Do you have a word for this or an image? What feelings are you experiencing?

Do you know what is seeking to be born in you? Is it tangible? Has it a shape? a color? a scent? What emotions do you feel?

Now we move into the next stage of blossoming which, however brief, impacts on our ability to accept and allow ourselves to shine. Do we allow others to shine or are we envious of their ability to do so with such charm and beauty?

Chapter 6

Late Spring: Blossoming

'How did that happen?' the small child asked, pointing at the blossom on the cherry tree.

'Well, it just grew out,' the adult replied.

'But how did it get out? How?' asked the child, tugging at the branch excitedly, sending pink cascades whirling across the pavement. 'How did it get out of the wood?'

'Well — first it became a bud, then the bud opened and out grew the flower....' the adult explained patiently.

But still the child's question lay unanswered. The child wanted to know how color, fragrance and such soft petals came out of the hard grey wood.

That child was me!

I still marvel each time I see the abundance of blossom crowning the cherry and apple trees each year; colors ranging from impossible bright cerise to soft pink and white. And after this sudden, yet brief burst of sylvan confetti come the majestic candles of chestnut released from winter, long sticky fists, and laburnum florets hanging like lemon icicles. On and on the blossoming spreads as if a fuse has been lit, igniting the country in colored flame. And I think, 'It's too much... stop the clock !' But then the May Queen enters, sweeping vast wedding confetti of creamy hawthorn across the fields, then elderflower. And all the time the gorse burns gold.....Its sweet coconut and vanilla fragrance mingling with the sharp musk of hawthorn.

I have learned to ask less questions from humans and more of nature itself. The fact is, blossoming is a miracle! It is a gift, a blessing.

The blossom is the icing on the cake. It is the 'bliss' the late mythologist, Joseph Campbell talked about. It is the wedding and the honeymoon. It is the falling in-love phase where we become enchanted by each other and life. It is the 'Ah-Ha' which Betty Edwards explains so well in her book; *Drawing on the Artist Within*. She describes it as the moment of illumination in any creative process. It is intensely happy and blissful. When Einstein reflected on the creative moment after he grasped the concept of gravity, he described it as; '...the happiest moment in my life.'

Blossoming is part of the process of the tree, of the flower, of life itself. It usually follows a period of waiting, of inner imprisonment, a period where a breakthrough has been made. It is the runner's high when he hits the endorphins; the mountaineer's triumph of having at last reached the summit. It is the ultimate experience. It takes us out of the mundane and into the realm of the miraculous and the transcendental. It heals, energizes, frees, transmutes and sets the vision for the future. Like deep pain or suffering, bliss is transformative. It is heady, lucid, and hypnotic all at the same time. Bliss is life's natural opiate where one half of the human population are struggling to reach, and the other half runs away from.

Blossoming can happen within a golden tipped instant as in the case of sudden insight, a breakthrough or vision as in the spiritual experience of many mystics, poets, artists, and scientists such as Einstein or James Lovelock when he had the Gaia hypothesis: 'like a flash of enlightenment'. The deeper and more intense the experience, the more far-reaching the results. Bliss experiences or blossoming can be life changing events because they communicate directly to the soul. We may in those razor-edged moments understand what our purpose for being here is. We see clearly, we aspire – we are as dragonflies with prismatic vision, able to fly backwards and forwards, as well as perceive multitudinous facets to each thought and dream. Dragonflies which, before this breakthrough, were larvae crawling at the bottom of muddy ponds, for weeks, months, years, hardly daring to dream, let alone envision the future.

Blossoming can last longer and manifest as a period within the life where events seem to flow towards us. Our work and progress within the world may seem effortless, blessed and full of opportunity. It is as if the world has come to the door and is waiting to shower us with countless gifts. We feel at peace with ourselves; both our past and our future are held in a golden glow. In retrospect, we suddenly perceive the meaning behind our experiences. We are full of genuine praise and admiration for the vast pattern of life. Our future unrolls before us strewn with infinite possibilities.

I was privileged to come to know an artist who had been in prison twenty years and remember the absolute joy he experienced when, after his release, he was able to walk on the grass again in bare feet. He was full of wonder and it seemed that the World Soul were ministering to him from all directions. He took a degree in art and although he did not have any money to support himself, the accommodation and all the grants he needed came to him. Opportunities abounded for him to paint and display his work, including restaurant ceilings, pub walls and private enterprises. In my lounge is a stunning oil painting of a dryad-like figure, half tree, half woman, aptly called 'Tree Goddess'. I had admired it so much that he had given it to me. Writing this I think of the artist, and feel an immediate connection with his soul.

This was the honeymoon period. During his long internment, he had given birth to a process of new life. His *Long Wait* had lasted years and he had ample time for contemplation, aspiration and reflection. It was in prison, he told me, that he had learned to meditate and established the firm foundations of an inner sanctuary.

Crazy though it may seem, many of us are afraid to blossom. Afraid to let ourselves go too high in case ...

In case of what?

In case we lose control? or are catapulted out into space somewhere, and not able to return to our normal and boring state. Sadly, as blossoming is as crucial a part of the process as any other stage, it cannot be avoided – not if we are going to realize our potential to the full.

Yet – how many of us do live our potential to the full? We complain about our life not being exciting, fulfilling or empowering enough, then run a mile when the golden opportunity presents itself, not just once, but again and again. We mutter about commitments, responsibilities and return to safety wherever that may be!

A word of warning though..... Unlived potential becomes resentful, frustrated and restless. It will not let us go. It haunts us through other people's lives *who do* realize their potential. These sickeningly fulfilled people keep waltzing across our path 'trailing clouds of glory' as they come, as if they were sent along to torment us on our unlived purpose. The fact is, our unrealized potential is inviting them to come and live by their example. No sooner do we meet a true 'soul mate' in the form of another unfulfilled 'poor me' person and get to like them and are prepared to share martyred lives together, then off they go wanting to live out and realize their full potential, inviting us to do the same!

Then there are our children. We do not hold them back – like we believe our parents did. We herd them out into the world to fulfill their potential, through school, college, university, or some secure and prestigious company. The only problem is that we send them out to fulfill *our* potential, not *theirs*. We call it sacrifice; our children call it bribery and end up hating us for it. We are afraid that our children will fail and make the same mistake as we did. Our children become afraid that we will withdraw our love if they do not do what we want. But since love is unconditional, love does not enter into it. No wonder our children rebel against us, disappoint us, fall by the wayside. And later, if they have any sense at all, fulfill their own potential amidst so many risks and pitfalls it puts us to shame.

It can never work out, this projection onto our children of our unrealized desires. They have their own calling, whatever it may be, and they cannot wear our moccasins for us.

So we need to embrace that blossoming period, brief though it may be. We need to lose control, desperately so and, unlearn whatever we have learned and held to be true. We need to let go of our crumbling securities and touch into the spontaneity we had when we were young, very young. If we cannot blossom, we cannot bear fruit. It is as simple as that. We cannot give if we have not allowed ourselves to receive. In essence, true giving is true receiving; for we become the container to hold life. If you feel you want to serve and make the world a better place, you have to start with yourself, and accept that like everyone else you need to be needed. It is fine to want to be needed, as long as we admit to it, otherwise we become one of those self-righteous do-gooders that everyone resents. True giving comes from the heart.

One of the most insistent viruses which can clog our system and prevent us from entering into bliss, is the thought that we are being too indulgent, becoming too preoccupied with ourselves. We might have been told this by a somewhat martyred parental or religious authority or simply by a jealous friend, brother or sister. Consequently, we might feel so infested with guilt at the prospect of having a 'wild' simply glorious time, that we cannot allow ourselves to enjoy anything. But if ejaculation did not occur there would be no babies, no continuity in the life cycles. If pollination did not occur, there would be no fruit. Orgasms and climaxes are an integral part of creation and vital to our life development.

And that's the whole point of our existence here, to be creative and bear fruit. But not just physical fruit, like flesh and blood babies and material acquisitions that are measured on a monetary level, but *soul* fruit, wisdom. Fruit that can be passed onto our greater family; to the world that bore us, our gift to the Great Mother.

The wonderful thing about blossoming is that it is not just for us. It is for the world. Blossoming is an act of service. Everyone enjoys being showered by blossom, everyone notices. Everyone is magnetized by it. People in blossom draw admirers, followers, fans, pupils, supporters and lovers. The world makes them into stars; star fruits. Everyone is energized by someone in blossom. Because it is soul blossom, it stirs the souls of others so that they feel inspired and encouraged. It is pure darshan to be in the presence of anyone in blossom. It is like being a caterpillar in the presence of a butterfly. It gives us permission to be – to be us. No one else can be us any more than we can be anyone else, or a hawthorn can be an oak tree. Our blossom is unique.

People in blossom motivate people to a cause. Blossom leads, it trails scented and colored petals wherever it goes. If you have ever been touched by anyone in blossom, whether physically, visually or verbally you will remember the attraction, the tremendous magnetism, as if they were reaching into your innermost centre and stirring up all the dreams and ideals you had laid to waste. People in blossom give others direction and 'courage' which comes from 'cour' the Latin word for heart. We all affect one another. And furthermore, blossoming is contagious. It ricochets around us, triggering off an explosion of blossoming. In nature, blossoming happens all at once. Nature blossoms in unison, or dynamic sequence. Watch the summer sports, tennis, hockey, football and see how they inspire others to realize their talents from the nations they represent. Look at Pop

Idol and all those gifted unknowns that suddenly emerge on centre stage, living out their dream and our dreams. Gifted unknowns like Susan Boyle who simultaneously stunned us with her voice and yet stung us with her ordinary humanness; a middle aged woman whom we could not put on a pedal stool because she had the same fears that we had. Then, a short while ago, another pop idol exited the stage of life in the form of Michael Jackson, certainly a colorful icon of my growing up, trailing media coverage behind him. What had all that monetary wealth given him but the tools to drastically change his facial appearance in a most bizarre way? The blossom had fallen, revealing the fruits of pain swelling beneath. Similarly, world fashions blossom in and out of vogue, rarely lasting more than a few weeks or months. Currently, computers are in full blossom, along with digital cameras and anything digital. Then there are I-pods, blue-ray networking, global communications. Next, we will replace electricity with light. We know how to do it. But we do not know how to charge for it because it is free. And how does the world get round that?!! Communications are flowering on the non technological front too. In the New Age milieu, orbs, earth healing and accompanying angels are blossoming.

We tend to think that in isolation, we have very little impact. But we never bloom in isolation; just as a tree never grows in isolation, however cut off it is from others in forests and woods. It is part of a vast company of trees worldwide. In isolation it becomes a representative of its kind, its race. Where a single tree has been allowed to grow in a field, it has a presence that can be felt, experienced from quite a distance. It commands the field. And when it blossoms, everyone notices. Everyone partakes of its beauty in whatever way they can: driving to work each morning, taking the dog for a walk, gazing through the window of the train, a bus. That single tree enters our hungry lives, trans-forming, enthusing, enlivening our sense of continuity and hope with its silent language. A communication takes place between tree spirit and human soul, and we feel uplifted, strengthened. Simply by being, it conveys much. It has come through the winter, emerged from the dead time and is remarried to life again.

We cannot know the effect we have on others when we are in blossom. That is not for us to see. By blossoming, we are indulging our potential by allowing ourselves to be. By our being, we give others permission to be in blossom too. We do not have to set an example, but *be* an example. The late Diana, Princess of Wales, was a compelling example of someone in blossom. She was just herself, living and fulfilling what she believed in and following her heart. Everywhere she went she left her fragrance, her love, her healing petals. She could not help it. How was she to know that she was to bring not just a nation to their knees at her death, but the whole world? And because she was overflowing with blossom, her fruits were many. She left a whole legacy of fruit and saplings behind for others to attend. She followed no one, only her heart. She was herself and look what she achieved by following her heart? She affected everyone and of course there were people who opposed her because her presence only reminded them of their unfulfilled potential. Throughout history, great innovations and changes benefiting mankind have been made by people in blossom. Diana was a modern day one.

Because, during this time of blossoming, we are lifted high above the mundane, we are empowered by a force or consciousness greater than ourselves. This is what mystics and psychologists refer to as the transpersonal or transcendental. We are literally saturated with creative potential. It is a fragrance coming off us, an indefinable color that attracts and draws the right people, like honey bees to collect nectar and draw inspiration from.

Basically this blossoming period is the impetus, the driving force which will carry us into our future. It instills in us a sense of surety, an unshakeable surety that we are on the right track, following the right career, writing the book we need to write, with the right partner. And in a sense this is true. We are following the right career, in the right place at the right time with the right person, although later on in the process when we are tried and tested by the elements, we might have our doubts. We might doubt our journey and even question all that we experienced and felt during our time of blossoming. And the only way we can get back to that state of enlightened knowing is through our centre, not through the head and brain. With our heart, we can always find our way back to the centre. The heart knows, the heart remembers because the heart is where the blossom is. Trees have heartwood, the inner centre which can completely dissolve away, leaving the tree hollow without harming the tree at all. Many old yew trees are hollow.

Because of the blossom's connection with the heart, understandably the blossoming period also has a lot to do with love and being in love; like the newly-wed brides showered with confetti and blessings. We fall in love and we see through the eyes of love. The world says we are looking through rose tinted glasses when in fact we are looking through real eyes, we are realizing or 'real eyeing' the beauty of another's soul and are in love with it.

A honeymoon period in life, of any kind, usually lasts about a year – a year and a day in the old lore. Wonderful though it is, we cannot stay in the honeymoon period for ever. The process has to move on; the blossom has to fall in order to continue in the process. When we are in love with someone our energies are going towards each other all the time, we are not that practical and just as the tree's purpose is to serve life, it is our purpose too. We have to share what we have got, or create a work together in the form of a human or creative child.

The blossom falls and, gradually, we begin to feel in contact with the earth again. There can be disappointment, a falling from grace, if this grounding process is not fully understood. If we cannot see that the blossoming is part of a greater cycle of maturing and commitment, we cannot move along the trajectory of another cycle. We become trapped, even imprisoned within the loss of the blossom and the need to return to it. We regress instead of progress. The blossoming is part of a greater cycle of maturing and commitment. Commitment itself is a soul quality, but in the young soul and indeed in the young person commitment may not be what is wanted. That is why one never forgets one's first love, the first blossom always inscribes itself indelibly across the heart.

Lost in the euphoria of our own blossoming, the in-love phase whether it be with a partner, a career, a book we are writing or a project we are undertaking, we do not consider the future. We are caught like moths to a flame in the illumination of the present moment.

As the blossom scatters upon the first breezes, we need to hold fast to our centre and in that is found the realisation that we are preparing for the next part of the process. Once we can see this and not become caught up in the 'loss' itself, we can look forward to the rest of the process with hope and anticipation.

Visualisation Exercise

Imagine a beautiful flower, like a peony or rose suddenly bursting into bud. The crumpled leaves falling open before your eyes. If you listen carefully to the world of your inner senses you might hear a barely audible 'pop' as the petals open. Breathe in with joy as you catch the subtle scent wafting across to you. Breathe out with relief as you experience the freedom of what was clenched and pent-up surrendering to the tension of becoming itself.

This can be used where there is a longing to realize your full potential. It helps to align you with your soul's purpose and bring it into consciousness, subsequently working through any barriers that may deflect you from your quest. Remember, the nearer you are to your soul's purpose and unlocking the treasure it has for you, the more dragons in the form of nameless fears rise up to test you and put you off. Don't be discouraged, press on!

Meditation

Be aware of the light which is the creative principle in the form of the sun, shining above you. As you focus on the light, its warmth and acceptance of you just as you are, gradually breathe this sun into your body. Imagine yourself breathing in the light, drawing it down like golden liquid, through the crown of your head and into your lungs. Let it rest there in your chest, at your heart centre. Focus on your need or longing which may be a dream that you have always had but never been able to realize. Do not worry if this longing is not accessible on a conscious level, it will still be there in some form or other. Perhaps it is quite nebulous, like a longing for freedom or creative expression of some kind. Perhaps it is a longing for a greater sense of unity or belonging in the world or a need to feel nourished on a spiritual level.

As you focus on your heart, be aware of the warmth and light that glows in it, and also the feelings which may arise like joy, wistfulness, excitement, love, sadness, etc. Don't push these feelings away even when they seem overwhelming or too much to bear. Know that it is at the point of greatest pressure that a breakthrough can occur. Alternatively, you might experience a deep peace as you step into sacred space, soul space.

Focusing on your heart and, using your inner vision become aware of a rosebud. Gradually see the petals unfolding in slow motion. Be aware of the color of the petals; their satin softness, the fragrance as the rose opens. Feel the connection between your heart and the rose. Experience your whole being opening and becoming receptive to the rose and rest in this consciousness for a while, knowing that this is your rose, your unfolding. Perhaps the rose has a message for you at this time in your life. Reach out to receive the wisdom in that message....

In your own time, gradually withdraw from the consciousness of the rose, knowing that it is there in your heart whenever you feel the need to make contact with it. Once again be aware of the light that sustains and feeds all creation then return to ordinary waking consciousness and make contact with your body.

Write down any insights you may have received, together with feelings and thoughts that may have been evoked. Release any blocked sensation within you in the form of a picture, use crayons and colors to express yourself and further ground the insight.

In the next chapter we look at our ability to commit ourselves to a work or chosen path. As each commitment demands sacrifices, it also tests our ability to hold on, stick at a project, a relationship when the going is tough.

Chapter 7

Summer: Ripening

The last of the white cascades of blossom had left the tree, forming soft pastel pools on the ground beneath. These seemed to possess a life of their own as invisible hands seized up the flurry of blossom, then cast it back to the ground again to form another pool. The drone of the bees which had thrummed the air only days before, had gradually subsided as the bees left looking for more pollen. The tree bereft of its white lace, looked quite ordinary again. But...A closer look revealed miniature fists of fruit. These were to grow and mature over the coming weeks, becoming large and succulent. The spadework had been done, the visitors would be back again later when the fruit was ready....

Our lives are all about bearing fruit, being productive and creative. Our language is deeply embedded with phrases which reflect our need and yearning to be profitable. We talk about projects 'bearing fruit' or 'becoming fruitful'; of allowing ideas to mature or ripen. We refer to investments being fruitful or even becoming barren. Ideas are seeds which we plant in the framework of a group, a system or company, hoping that they will germinate and spread. Success is fruitfulness, where products multiply and expand. The Biblical term in the Old Testament 'Be fruitful and multiply' has been a template we have followed to excess with our world population. Fruitfulness is expressed in modern day terms as branches, offshoots of the original tree.

Sadly, the age we live in where natural processes are hurried along, often with dire consequences; we strip the whole ripening process of its most vital ingredient which is time.

Although we may believe we are able to genetically engineer crops to produce successful fruit and with modern technology simulate the seasons, we cannot genetically engineer the soul. The soul needs time and patience to incubate, grow and expand. It also needs our diligence and dedication to its growth and development.

The 'fruit' may be explicit in the form of an apprenticeship of sorts, waiting for the birth of a child, training for a career in the arts, medicine, education or law. Alternately, the fruit can be implicit in the form of an initiation which, like pregnancy, are rarely short lived. We might find ourselves caring for an elderly relative, a handicapped child or starting a business. Waiting for a business or project to bear fruit is risky. In fact all long term ventures are risky with no real guarantees. But if we do not take that initial risk, we will never know or gain valuable insight into the process of living through a pregnancy with all its longings and disappointments. There are many who talk about doing this, but few who dare to do it. If we cannot feel a sense of dedication or destiny, then it is unlikely we will wait for our project to bear fruit. It will feel too much like hard work, rather than a positive investment of time and energy.

During the blossoming cycle we have fallen in love with our goal. We will have partnered it and loved it enough to tackle any obstacles which might arise in the process. Bliss, although seemingly 'ungrounded', is the actual *tap root* to our process. That is why if a tree fails to blossom, then it will not bear fruit. Since everything in nature is a process, bliss is such a vital part that without it the process cannot fully be consummated.

Nothing can remain the same. The honeymoon period must end just as the blossom must fall and that tiny nodule of fruit swell into its potential. Everything expands or breaks down according to the polarities of life and death, and resurrection is the bridge between the two. The blossom is brief and vital, yet like a wedding it is life changing. After the blossom fades we have to take a step forward of dedication and commitment, or at least be willing to do that. We cannot be 'blissed-out' or 'in love' all the time. Wonderful though it is, we would never get any work done! We have to finish the process and understand that it is cyclical. The bliss will come again, but often after a period of hard work and relentless dedication.

To examine our part in the process, we have to remember that the fruit is part of the tree that sustains it. If it breaks off from the tree before it is ripe, it shrivels up and dies. It is too young, too immature to ripen on its own. While we belong to a framework, whether it be a university, a marriage or law school, we are connected to it. The university, marriage, law school, sustains us in order that we can grow and produce. It feeds us; either by offering a salary, accommodation, tuition, paying our insurance, providing us with a pension scheme or, most important of all, love and acceptance. The continuity of our survival and maturity depend on the organization we are part of. This again is reflected in our language when we say we work for a 'branch' of a company or we are looking at our 'family tree'. It is through our *connectivity* that we grow in strength, breadth and width. And although we may feel our individuality is submerged and we lack a strong sense of self so that we vanish into the masses, the fruit we are tending is nurturing the strength needed to assert individuality. Apprentices grow into their completed role as pregnant young women grow into mothers. It does not matter that you have never graduated or become a mother or father before. By bearing the wait or 'weight' of your expectations you will become all that you dreamed and more. It does not matter that you feel inadequate and 'green', the fruit will mature in the light of the world. The harvest will come whether you like it or not and green apples will become flushed and ripe. As the apple contains the pips for new growth, new life, so do we bear the seeds of continuity and further production on an individual level. But until then we *need* the company, the career, the marriage, the whole system as the system *needs* us. Systems work even if not always in the way we would like them to work. If they did not work, they would no longer be systems.

As in all the tree's cycles we need to touch into the various levels it is operating on. Sometimes we can become so preoccupied with the fruit, we forget about the rest of the tree: the tap root, the heartwood, the sap which is its life force and energy. Ironically, the more we are able to perceive ourselves as an integral part of the whole, the more we *enable* ourselves to establish our individuality.

Probably most of us remember times when we dropped out of careers or abandoned projects and relationships. If it was not through personal choice, we may feel sad, resentful even angry about this. Perhaps circumstances did not allow us to continue with the career or our education. Perhaps the job or marriage was not all that we thought it would be. Maybe we were not ready to cope with such an undertaking. Something stronger may have called us away to live out another experience which seemed to make more sense at the time. Perhaps we dropped out and then, at a later date, took it up again and completed it because the time and environment were right.

Perhaps you can take a bit of time out and reflect through your life at projects and relationships that have been aborted or left incomplete.

How do you feel about them now? What sort of feelings does this evoke in you? What can you do about it? Can you think of anything positive which has emerged instead through this experience?

I know from my own personal experience, that I have had regrets about not having pursued a promising sports career. Circumstances had not allowed me to continue my athletic activities even though I got in to the trials for the 'All England' at sixteen, just before I left school. Consequently, I emerged into early adult life, not feeling adequate, especially academically. Studying later in life has, fortunately, mitigated these feelings of failure and, in retrospect, I can see that through the shortcomings life dealt me in the form of illness, I was able to develop my creativity. A wealth of creativity and art are spoiled by too much dissection, criticism and, basically, over education. Yet having experienced being the fruit that broke off from the tree before I was mature, I understand the difficulties of going it alone, not having the support of the main tree. Feelings of isolation and inadequacy can wear away at self-esteem and whittle down the personality defenses. Even though this creates the ideal opportunity for 'soul' to break through and make its presence known, this does not always help at the time.

Exiling yourself from a supportive framework is an experience that can only be understood if it is undergone. It is easy to judge, but a lot less easy to empathize and understand the reasons why.

And yet, it is through the final separation from the main tree that the fruit is harvested. And it is through separation that the new tree grows. In different aspects of the tree's cycle, separation is equally as important as connectivity.

The ripening process is a rich time in our lives.

It is a time of accumulating knowledge, wisdom, power, resources for the future. It cannot be hurried or bypassed, but it *can* be enjoyed! After all, it is the most creative thing we can do with our lives. Ripening is also about taking responsibility for our project, for what we are manifesting in our lives. It is not about blaming others if things fail to develop the way we want them to. It is not expecting others to carry us through when things get difficult or to do the work for us. Our attitude towards ripening can give us valuable feedback on how we feel about responsibility; where we put the blame and the praise.

How do you feel about bearing fruit?

Can you think about any projects which have borne fruit in your life?

Do you find it hard to stick things out once you have begun them?

Do you abandon projects halfway through? Why?

Is it because of impatience, or is it a fear of success or achievement or responsibility?

How do you feel about responsibility and commitment in general? What are your areas of responsibility? Do you enjoy these?

As some of us will find the fruiting process can offer up challenges which, at the time, we feel unable to fulfill and are tempted to run away from, still others will take great pride in their ability to achieve and manifest. Responsibility goes hand in hand with personal power. If we cannot realize our personal power and own it, responsibility will always be a source of conflict. To the other extreme, some of us will want to bear fruit all the time and consequently exhaust the whole process.

Is your sense of self-worth dependent on how much you can achieve, do and give?

Are you an achiever, an over- achiever perhaps?

Do you find fallow periods difficult?

Meditation

Be aware of yourself as a tight nodule of fruit. Feel the safety in the compact structure, the varnished outer layer of skin that protects your innermost core. Experience the potential you hold to swell, grow and become fully this fruit. Experience the warmth of the morning sun upon you, drying the dew. You feel the impulse to become more fully yourself, to reach all your potential. Experience your individuality, but also yourself being part of the tree that birthed you, the strong branches that hold you and through which you draw your nourishment. In your time of pregnancy, experience yourself not just as an individual, but part of something much greater that holds the template of all you can and will be.

Experience the joy and wonder of being pregnant.
Relax into being in this place of quiet potential and waiting.
Is there a message for you at this time?

When you feel ready, bring yourself slowly back and ground your insights by writing about what you have experienced or by drawing or coloring.

We now move onto the next chapter, *Harvest*, which is the completion of the cycle from bud to fruit. Such a time may evoke feelings of relief or loss, or both even, and wondering what next? Harvest is about the Ameri-Indian give away and how this may impact on our need to hang onto conditions, rather than release them for the good of all. Additionally, we may be afraid of rejection and this may damn up our natural spontaneity. How easy is it to let go, now that we have got so used to holding on and holding out ?

Chapter 8

Late Summer: Harvest

The tree's boughs were heavy with fruit. As the sun's rays caught the dew on the apples, they glistened in the morning. A gust of wind shook the tree and an apple fell, bruising its ripe flesh on the ground. Within moments, the insects alighted on it, beginning to suck at the sweet juice. Another apple fell, and another. It was time to harvest the season's fruit that had ripened in the sun, wind and rain. That which had fallen on the ground would not be wasted. At night the hedgehogs and foxes would eat the fruit, and what was left in the morning would be shared by the wasps and the birds...

Harvest is the completion of the cycle. What has been conceived in the spring has blossomed and borne fruit. Our projects, our children and careers have swelled out into their full potential. They have reached the limit of their growth in that direction. They have reached their prime, their zenith. All the work, dedication and sacrifices that we have made have finally paid off.

A number of feelings may come up during the completion of this cycle. First and foremost there will be a sense of relief and pride in the achievement. We no longer have the stress of 'holding fast' any more. The task, the project has been completed. We are free at last. And this release from months and years of commitment can be almost euphoric. The children have made it on their own. They no longer need us. The tree and fruit are free from each other. But....

Every mother and every child knows it is not as easy as that. As the fruit carries the seeds of the mother tree within it, the child carries the genes and memories of the parent. Similarly, our career, or where we have trained, the project we have poured our energy into or the painting or book that we have borne, carries a part of us within it. All offspring, however they manifest, contain a part of their creator within them in the form of their physical parent and divine parent. So this is why the child can often feel a compulsion to live out the dreams of their physical parent; because they contain the psychic residue of their parent's dream which, itself, might have been the shared memory of their ancestral lineage. Similarly, they carry genes of their ancestors which may be hardwired to live out this dream. Whether they want to fulfill their parents dream or not, or are even conscious of it, extricating themselves from this ancestral lineage or dream will be hard. Additionally, there may be issues of guilt around following their own path rather than their parent's. This is especially difficult if the parent has a lot of denial around their unlived potential and consequently hides behind a self-sacrificing persona. There will be a lot of unconscious material accompanying their desires and ambitions if different from their parents. But, do we really know what drives us unconsciously to perform certain acts? The nurture versus nature theory still goes on today. Some of us have a strong sense of destiny and this may go against all parental injunctions and even free will. How do we make the distinction between the internal forces within us that emanate from our divine parent and blood parent? Are they even the same? Drives are powerful and are unconscious until we have enough insight to challenge them. We may not have a template of our maturity in the form of the apple or oak tree, other than being a human being, but we do have a quest to fulfill our potential. The clue to figuring out what this quest may be, lies in following our heart rather than fleeting desires or thoughts that emanate solely from the desire and mental level. The heart may be in conflict with the mind, or they may be the same which is a wonderful confirmation that you are following the right threads.

At this point it is probably good to take a little time out to examine your own feelings and experiences around this.

How much of this do you think applies to you?

Do you feel you are living out the dream of your parents?

If you are, are you happy doing this?

If so, then it is not a problem. Be happy that you share the same dreams. Have you had to fight for what you want to be or do and feel that you have not been accepted by your parents for this?

Perhaps you need help in letting this go and discovering your own needs.

How do you feel about your own children? Are you aware of the under-lying reasons for what you want for them? Have you asked them what they want?

If you find that you are trapped in this dream-fulfillment cycle inherited from your parents and probably their parents too and, now, perhaps visited on your own children, be assured that, if you want, you have the power to change this. Seeing the truth, painful and uncomfortable though it may be initially, can be very freeing. Identifying and grasping the reality can empower you to move on to create a new life pattern independent of the family cycle. It is never too late.

As the previous cycle of ripening is about holding on, commitment, dedication, sticking it out, harvest is all about letting go and release.

It is no surprise that the North American Indians referred to it as the Give-away time; for it is also about giving and service.

Unless we can fully release our fruit, whether they are in the form of our children or other projects, we cannot give them away. If we cannot give them away, the once symbiotic relationship turns sour because it has outlived its usefulness. The fruit left on the tree turns rotten. The tree can no longer support it and has nothing more to give. Failure to give away, release and let go invites the rot to set in. Decay and breakdown mark the complementary edge to the creative process.

Additionally, if we cannot 'give away', we have no space for fresh input. Giving and receiving cannot survive without each other. Nothing exemplifies this so well as the tree and the whole plant family in general. For a tree to produce fruit it has to take in water, sunlight and minerals. If the tree is deprived of any of these, its fruit is poor and even non existent. Within this lies an important lesson for people who give a lot, for the *givers* of the world to understand that they *must take time* to imbibe of sustenance too, or else they quickly become burnt-out and exhausted. Similarly people that are predominantly *receivers* need to understand that the essence of true giving is receiving. True giving is being able to receive. Then there are the *spongers* who take for the sake of it and hold back from giving. In holding back their gifts, even the humility and grace with which to receive, they deny themselves what they most want to have, self-empowerment and dignity. *Spongers* feel that the world owes them a living and want to get as much as they can for as little as possible. This sort of 'poverty consciousness' is self-fulfilling and not a particularly pleasant experience for the *giver* or *sponger*.

Giving and receiving communicate a universal language and work the world over. What you put into life comes back to you sooner or later. What you hold back from life returns to you too, often as emotional anguish and regret. Every entrepreneur knows that money is not amassed by hoarding, but rather by a subtle interplay of investment and risk taking. Money is a living force which comes from the same root word as 'blood'. It needs to circulate or the system clogs up, it becomes bad.

Investment is spending with a purpose. Spending for its own sake is just frittering away resources which is a form of financial hemorrhaging.

I have come across many people who tithe; that is who give away ten percent of their total income to a work of a spiritual nature. This is the true essence of give-away and harvest. This does not mean giving *everything* away which is ultimately just as bad as giving nothing away. It means giving away proportionally to what we have. What I have learned from these people who tithe often over a period of ten, twenty, thirty years, is that the money they give away *always* comes back to them through other sources. Often it doubles or multiplies. I have heard this from once cynical business men and women who have begun to tithe just to try out the process. It does not matter what your beliefs are, it works.

It *does* work.

On a smaller scale, I find that what I give out returns to me. The more broke I am when I give money away, the quicker it returns and it frequently multiplies. I don't give money away for this reason. I give it away because I *trust* that my needs will be met according to the law of life, or Divine Law.

Some years ago, I gave ten pounds I could ill afford to a lady who dedicates her life looking after stray cats. I knew she needed it more than me at Christmas. Three days later I learned that I had won first prize in an RSPCA animal poetry competition. The prize was forty pounds. The money had multiplied four-fold!

If you trust this divine flow and do not abuse it, your needs are always met.

Around the same time period, I was desperate for a holiday and I had an opportunity to go to Norway. The fare to Oslo was two hundred pounds. I barely had that to last me until the end of the month for food and bills, but I also knew how much I needed that break. So against all odds, I decided to go, even though I knew I did not have enough money for the fare. The very next day, propped up outside the front door, because the postman could not get it in the letter box, was a package from the United States based Blue Mountain Arts publishing company. It contained a complimentary packet of fifty poetry cards and a check for three hundred dollars in payment for one of my poems! This was not something I could possibly have expected as I had submitted the poetry over two years previously and forgotten all about it.

It works.

But harvest and give-away by their very nature, demand trust and risk. We have to be willing to *risk* what we *have* and *trust* that our *needs* will be taken care of. For many of us living in the confines of the Western World where risk, especially financial risk is fear based, it is a very hard thing for us to do. By cutting ourselves off from the language of nature and the use of intuition, we have developed a limited vision which leaves little room for the unconditional, the miraculous and the Great Mystery of life.

But life is risk. If we do not risk, then we do not fully live and a life half lived yields a very unpalatable fruit. In fact, our lives can be so devoid of risk, with comfortable cushions situated below any precipices that might loom up in the form of various insurance policies which flood our culture, that we will actually pay for risk, for the thrill of it. We go on organized risky holidays, skiing down slopes or trekking in the Himalayas in order to experience a sense of thrill again. We were made for risk — risk is growth.

Here I want to introduce Henry Thomas Hamblin, a practical mystic who based his whole life and work on risk. To give a little background, he was a highly successful business man working in London as an optician in the 1920s. Affected very deeply by the death of his young son, he gave up the business he had built up in London and put everything into buying a house in Sussex. There, he set up a magazine based on positive thinking and developing one's spiritual vision. He had no staff at the beginning that he could pay and no real experience of publishing, writing or editing and when challenged about this, he replied: 'I always teach best what I need to learn – and I have a lot to learn!'

His magazine, *The Science of Thought Review*, was to have a circulation of 12,000 with readers all over the world. This magazine then was one of the first of its kind in Britain and attracted enough readers to run a series of courses on positive thinking which were to be highly popular too. The incredible thing was that he ran the whole project on trust, giving a lot of his material away, never asking for money, only stating his needs. He was to attract writers like Henry Victor Morgan and Joel Goldsmith in the States who inspired by his vision, went on to develop magazines of their own. I took over the running of this magazine in 1994 and changed the name to *New Vision*. The magazine is still running today, forty years after he died, and still circulates largely on trust. What started out as a major risk has become a lifelong vision.

Henry Thomas Hamblin wrote some very good pieces on risk, and because they were based on his own life experience they still hold fast today.

He wrote:

If we feel that we have come to the end of a phase; that we have outgrown our present occupation and that we have the ability and necessary enthusiasm to start a new life, then I think that we should make the change. Of course, it will not be easy. It means living dangerously. It means risking our all financially, in order to gain freedom, spiritually.

Not everything returns that we give away – at least not in the form we expect or when we expect it too. It may return years later in another way, even decades later, or if you accept reincarnation, it can return in another life!

The word 'talent' which we equate with a creative gift, has its source in the Bible where it was believed to apply to money. Here a merchant gave money to his three servants. To the first he gave five, to the second two and to the third he gave one talent.

Recalling them some time later, he was pleased that the one he had given five talents had traded them for five more talents and the second had taken his two and traded them for two more but the servant with one talent had not dared take a risk and buried his and consequently it had been taken away from him as he was not deemed worthy of it.

Similarly, if creative talent is not used it dwindles away. The inspiration literally dries up. The talent is taken away.

Service is a word with a lot of innuendoes and pressures. I hated the word for years. It reminded me of 'do gooders' and sounded like a form of imprisonment, where your wings were clipped and you turned your life over to the army, nursing, church work or some other vocation. Even though I have been a clinical support worker for some years, I still rebel against the word 'service' as I rebelled against the label my profession gave me of being good and angelic. I was none of these things. It took me a long time and a lot of rebellion before I could free up all the negative paraphernalia I had built around the concept of service, and create a new one. Again, nature came to rescue me as I observed how her whole presence of being was a service to life itself. Nature was not a 'do gooder', she was just *being*. Her service was unconditional and joyful rather than self-righteous.

True service, I came to understand was an act of inner being. It is our true nature to serve each other; to give and receive. As we enter more fully into our true nature through meditation and prayer, service become unconditional and even joyful.

Now we come to the other part of the process; being able to receive. Children receive as they give spontaneously. It is a natural part of their consciousness and one of the first forms of behavior they learn.

There are times when we need to receive as there are times when we need to give, each is appropriate and as vital as breathing in and out. Women, especially, or rather the feminine part of our nature, finds it hard to receive. There is a lot of guilt attached to this which stems from years of having personal needs put on hold in order to serve the masculine. We can see this with the earth where all its resources have been exploited to excess and nature has been turned, even genetically engineered, into a huge production machine. Nature has had so much taken from her with a negligible amount returned, she is drying up. In some areas where she has been particularly abused, through chemicals, she cannot give any more. Her only recourse for survival is to draw on primeval elemental forces and use shock treatment in the form of droughts, floods and hurricanes.

Yet, despite all this repression, that which is denied, cut back, becomes even stronger. The feminine is finding a voice and being heard. The feminine is moving into the media, into the art world and especially computers. What was once a male dominated area is becoming female dominated.

On an individual level we need to receive, to breathe in, to allow ourselves time to express, relax, do our own thing and contemplate. If we do not, we become undernourished, drained and resentful. And our ability to give dries up. There is a saying that goes something like this; 'If you love something, then let it go, if it returns to you it was yours, if not it was never intended to be yours.'

Meditation

Be aware of the fruits you have harvested throughout this year/or over this passage of time.

They may not have been comfortable fruits to bear and tend.

You may even want to hold them, marvel at their firmness and the way in which they were first conceived. Thank them for all the insight they have given you through both testing and inspirational times.

Allow yourself to experience the strong feelings that connects them to you. And then let these feelings go. As you know, they carry your dreams as they journey into the world, understand that they also carry their own dreams and visions for their life.

When you feel ready, release them with love. Let them go....

We are now about to move from the cycle of visibility and production to a less visible one where, in outer worldly terms, there is less that is tangible, productive and of any value. But in real terms this is where the work at the personality level moves into soul making. The more challenging the winter cycle, the greater the soul work and the opportunity for deepening. The Fall marks the threshold, through the subliminal gateway to the *Long Wait.*

Chapter 9

The Fall: Stripping

Each of the tree's leaves were tipped with gold and veined with amber and red. It had long released its fruit and trembled as a barely percep-tible breeze began to stir, causing the dry leaves to rub against each other. Soon the breeze would gather to a wind which would wrestle and shake the branches until the leaves began to fall and whirl in a majestic dance of fire. A dance of celebration and loss. The tree could feel the new buds hidden beneath the turning leaves. Buds which, although sleeping, would waken in the spring and bring new life. Once again, the sap would rise, heralding the birth of another cycle. This was fall, the time of letting go and surrendering to the elements that had brought it into being. The fall was little less than an invitation to participate in the death that precedes resurrection and rebirth.

There are so many powerful elements taking place at this stage that they cannot be swept under the carpet as leaves often are! These elements focused on, as a whole, express an overriding sense of celebration, completion, transformation and excitement. It is a major, even majestic passage of transformation from apparent death to resurrection and rebirth. And yet...

...Too often the fall, and the stripping it brings, is viewed in a negative light, almost as if it is the end and that everything is lost. But since the cycle of the tree is eternal, nothing can ever be lost. It can only be transmuted into a higher order of life and reality. When we see the stripping in a negative way, we are simply overlooking the facts and failing to acknowledge the practical steps creating the process. We allow ourselves to become so caught up in the loss that it is impossible to focus on anything beyond this. We develop tunnel vision. We want to hold onto the leaves as we wanted to hold onto the fruit. We do not want them to fall because we are afraid of seeing nothing under the leaves rather than the buds — or perhaps we are *afraid* to see the *buds*. Afraid of the continuity they represent because it involves a change in our thinking.

Viewing an event in a simple practical way can often reduce the formidability of a situation and bring it closer to our understanding. Ignorance creates a brick wall of fear which is hard to break down. If we can *understand* the changes taking place within the tree, then we can relate to it and accept the identical processes that possess our own psyche.

The sap which is made up of water drawn up from the tree's roots, contain valuable soil nutrients. In the spring it rises to the top layers of the tree, fuelling the tree's growth and nourishment and beginning the photosynthesis in the leaves which harness the light. This sap is the tree's energy and life force; the tree's green blood, if you like. It rises up the tree through the sapwood which forms the outermost layer of the tree, between the heartwood and bark. In the fall, the sap is drawn back into the roots, draining away from the leaves. So the leaves, deprived of their life-force, begin to die. Nevertheless, the life force still remains in the tree, nourishing the roots, ready to rise again in the spring and begin the cycle all over again. By doing this the tree, like a computer, is closing down a lot of its circuits and running on as little energy as possible. The power is on, the tree is alive, but it is entering a state of rest from outer activity. In that period it can conserve its energy for a valuable healing and strengthening process to take place.

The falling leaves are not lost either. Through the process of decay where they are broken down into various components, they are transmuted into humus, which provide valuable nutrients for the soil – for the next cycle. Also the decaying leaves provide food for the earthworms which not only recycle the leaves, but also ventilate the soil allowing it to breathe. As the trees are the lungs of the planet, so are the humble earthworms, the lungs of the soil.

The stripping is literally the end of a cycle which heralds the beginning of another.

Leaves by their very nature speak of impermanence. They literally rise and fall. This impermanence reflects the transitory earthly conditions which we pass through. We come and we go. We leaf and fall, ebbing and flowing with the tides of being. This is the passage of life; as paths open and close around us, the scenery changes, shifts and transforms. Even the foundations upon which we build our seemingly solid structures alter, subside and change. Nothing is stable or permanent and the more solid and immovable we make our structures, the more vulnerable they are. A tree can bend in the storm and stretch its roots, a house hampered by its own inflexibility can be ripped apart as seasonal and global news confirms again and again.

Similarly, if we do not allow a certain elasticity within the beliefs we have about the world, they too can be subject to the same violent assaults. There is nothing wrong with our impermanence, only in our negation of it. Denial breeds fear. Acceptance and receptivity are the very components that lend pliability to a situation or state of being.

Life moves on… sometimes 'leaving' us behind.

The leaves have to fall to make way for the new buds. Young and small organizations are more open to change and expansion because it is the only way they can survive and fit into the already established structures. But older organizations, because of their past success, have a tendency to rest in the rather tenuous and false security that they are so solid and stable they do not need change. They forget that because they are part of life, they have to breathe in new ideas. Consequently, they become cut off from the life force, fail to breathe and suffocate on stale air. They have literally come and gone — and life takes over. It is dangerous to think that one is so big and invincible that one does not have to change. Ironically, that very awareness attracts change in large doses! We can see this in the collapse of huge banking organizations that have become too complacent about the inherent fallibility that underpins all matter. Recently, in the UK where various banks and members of Parliament have abused taxpayers' money to line their own private nests, have had to eat humble pie while their 'dirty laundry' has been relentlessly thrown out into the public arena. The saying 'as safe as houses' no longer applies in the midst of a global credit crunch. Emerging from all of this is the growing awareness that global systems are all interconnected. Abuse of resources in one area has a knock on effect in other areas. Plundering the rainforests for valuable timber, precious metals and wildlife that can be marketed, ultimately affects us all.

Back to the world of leaves which are being stripped from their branches and rustle and whisper as they fall and flutter from their moorings. When we talk of 'arriving' and 'coming,' we are able to visualize positive images such as the birth of a baby, a job, a career. We await the arrival of a child, a friend or visitor. We experience expectation, apprehension and excitement. Arrival, coming and becoming are usually positive in nature, filling us with optimism.

But when we talk of leaving and departure, we equate this with a sense of loss, absence — a wrenching away of the intimate and familiar. Something that once belonged to us, that which we loved and were closely connected with is going, departing, leaving. We can even experience this loss when difficult and unpleasant experiences actually *leave* us. They were, at least, familiar. They filled us, held us even if they represented conflicting processes within our lives. It seems incredible that we can grow so attached to our obstacles, yet most of us do, so that even when they leave us, we often unconsciously create new obstacles to take their place. Removal of obstacles brings freedom. Yet freedom, although sought after by most of us, can be a frightening terrain after a few weeks. It is also recognized to be one of our four greatest human fears beside annihilation, death and nonbeing. We become disorientated by its vastness where there seem to be none of the familiar boundaries which have shaped and divided our lives in the past. In fact, instead of bringing a release from responsibility, freedom brings us a greater responsibility – the responsibility of ourselves. With no tangible obstacles to blame we are forced to look into the mirror of ourselves. Freedom brings vistas of limitless potential that we can drown in. Our only defense is to pull back our energy, withdraw and become bored. We crave new experience *with* boundaries which, like young children and rebellious teenagers, we can test and push against. Yes, we do long for freedom, but in very small doses where we can believe we have some measure of control over it. Perhaps this is because we have little understanding of freedom. The clue to unlocking its meaning lies in the word itself; 'freedom', which comes from the same root word as Friday and the Nordic 'Freya's day.' And Freya is the Goddess of love and beauty. Until we can open ourselves more fully to love, the unconditional kind, we cannot possibly understand this vast country called freedom. Few have had the purity of intention to walk it. Those who have walked it, have often been ostracized and condemned in their time for bringing back its knowledge, yet, after their death been worshipped for ever after! Until we can open ourselves up to love and beauty and harness these qualities within ourselves, freedom will always seem unattainable, just out of reach. Love brings freedom – Freya's kingdom.

Back to the whole concept of departure and leaving.

Nothing ever really leaves us because when outer conditions and people depart from us, never to return, it is only because we have integrated their essence within us. When we have learned a difficult lesson, the problem or conflict leaves us – it's presence is no longer necessary for our growth; we have synthesized the conflicting conditions within our psyche. When we lose a loved one, whatever our beliefs, whether we believe in life after death, reincarnation or atheism, we will find the part they represented within us lives on. It has taken root. Walt Whitman, the American poet, expresses this whole concept within the first few lines of his poem; 'There Was a Child Went Forth':

There was a child went forth every day,
And the first object he looked upon and received with
wonder or pity or love or dread, that object he became,
And that object became part of him for the day or a certain
part of the day.......or for many years or stretching
cycles of years...

Likewise, the leaves fall because they have served their purpose as a part of the tree. The tree has synthesized the light and the leaves have harvested it and breathed their life-giving oxygen into our tired air.

True 'leaving' is an endless journeying because everywhere we go, we leave a part of ourselves behind. Whether we journey to the local shops, or to a holiday villa abroad or simply navigate the Internet, we leave something of ourselves there, either in the air we breathe, a fragrance, a footfall, epidermal cells, money or an e-mail address. And that calling card, whatever form it takes, becomes synthesized into information or another product. We shed bits of ourselves as we go which become integrated into the environment, recycled in some way.

Likewise, we become as we arrive and begin to open ourselves to the experience. The more we shed, the more we open ourselves. The more we open ourselves, the more we shed. Like the in-breath and out-breath they are interchangeable. This is *soul metabolism* and the rate at which we metabolize conditions and events, depends on the speed and level at which our consciousness vibrates.

Each time we say 'goodbye' to our friends and loved ones, we die a little to them. If and when we return to each other, we will never be quite the same again, neither will they. That is why we use the word 'goodbye'—'God be with you' — to remind each other of our true nature, our inner divinity which is the bond we share with all living creatures. And if we cannot recognize this core of essential being within ourselves, then how can we recognize it in others, *all* others not just family and friends? The falling of leaves reminds us of the cyclical processes we undergo in the metabolism of the soul.

In this context, I feel a need to bring in the importance and difficulty of letting go of beliefs. These beliefs may be about ourselves, the people around us or the world we live in. Often the most entrenched beliefs are the most resistant to being uncovered. This is understandable when we realize our understanding of the world is based largely on beliefs rather than direct knowledge. A belief serves us in the beginning by creating a sense of connection with the world or each other, but sometimes when beliefs have outlived their usefulness, they become destructive mindsets. Rather than keeping us safe, they keep us imprisoned. We can understand how resistant beliefs are when we see that, largely, ethnic wars are based on poorly informed beliefs. If we really believed in true brotherhood, we would seek to understand each other and include difference rather than use it as a line of division. Sometimes our beliefs can be so resistant that their presence jeopardizes any further growth, so that it takes something like a mental and emotional breakdown to initiate a much needed breakthrough in consciousness.

Sleep is sometimes known as the 'little death' and certainly the ritual of undressing to go to bed and taking our *leave* of the day, resembles the stripping cycle of the tree. We say, we fall asleep and 'come to' when we wake up. We fall, drop down and become. We go to sleep, die to the old in order to become new, renewed again. We all know that a long period without sleep removes our ability to become renewed, restored again.

And yet there is this shared sense of sadness in viewing the falling leaves on the tree, so unlike the sense of relief we might have as we fall asleep. Could this be because this touches into soul sadness? A distant memory that we all share of 'leaving the father's house' leaving a heavenly divine state in order to become birthed in the world. Does it somehow remind us of our own sense of exile in the world? A separation that took place long before leaving the mother's womb. An exile that initiates an endless searching for that state of completeness within the world, within other people as we seek to manifest that memory of unity in the world.

We have fallen, dropped down, but we have forgotten that in leaving one state, we are becoming and arriving at another, our true divine heritage. After the stripping there is always the becoming.

It might be good to examine how you feel about this natural cycle of falling leaves. What feelings does this evoke within you? How did you feel about this as a child? Have your feelings changed over the years? What are your memories?

Reflect over major points of departure in your life. This can be leaving home, college, a job, a marriage, letting go of children or a loved ones. What sort of feelings have these incidents evoked in you?

Can you find the strengths that were born out of these experiences?

We are passing through that liminal gateway into the winter period of the *Long Wait*. We are entering deeper into soul life where the everyday world, in contrast, can seem unreal and distant. Even though we may experience a sense of isolation and imprisonment, this is only in a worldly sense, we are actually united with forces and energies that are seeking to heal and transform us.

Chapter 10

Winter: The Long Wait

I said to my soul, be still, and wait without hope
For hope would be for the wrong thing; wait without love
for love would be love of the wrong thing; there is yet faith
But the faith and the love and the hope are all in the waiting.
T.S. Eliot

I am writing this in early November when the leaves have long left the trees and they stand naked and stark against the skyline. Although the buds for the spring have been present as far back as last fall, they will remain like that, wearing the rain and the snow until February through to April when the sap will rise to meet the growing warmth of the sun, teasing the buds open. The buds, although hidden in late summer, will have waited for their time to come for at least six months. Reflect on this for a moment: *waited for their time to come..*

For in this is held the secret of our life; our time held in ice until the thawing process is ready. And however much we want *our time to come*, there is nothing we can do to hurry it along. The waiting is as much a part of the process as what we want to emerge. Also, like you, I know the time *will* come when the buds open. We know this because it is part of our life experience. We have witnessed how seasons come and go, time and time again. The process is recorded on video, films, expressed in paintings, poetry and written in scientific books and journals. We would laugh if anyone tried to destabilize our surety of this. This is the process of nature. But for ourselves we feel this is different, somehow. Why?

Why should we think that our own individual process is different?

Are we not part of the biosphere and subject to the same natural laws? Is it because we feel we have more power over our environment than nature? Yet, if this was so, perhaps we should feel more sure about the conclusion of our waiting, rather than less sure?

We can perhaps argue that a seed from which the tree will emerge, has an inbuilt program which comes into operation the moment the seed makes a commitment to life by taking root. And this program is held within the matrix of nature and ensures the continuity of life through an annual cyclical process. But, because we do not believe that we have a similar program which is endeavoring to unfold within us, we cannot believe that we are subject to the same cyclical laws as nature. Yet... we *are* nature. We can argue that after the developmental process and physical maturation from child to adult, we act upon our environment by exerting will and choice. We are not embedded in the same matrix of nature like trees, plants and flowers. We do not have a sense of connectivity to nature other than depending on her for food, nourishment and oxygen. Yet, in actuality, we *are* totally dependent on nature from a survival level.

How would it be if we knew we have an inbuilt program that is ever struggling to unfold within us and that our will exerts itself in the freedom in choosing to yield to this or, alternatively, sabotage our soul's intention?

Jungian psychotherapist, James Hillman, explores this further in his seminal book, *The Soul's Code*, where the 'daimon' is the 'calling' we may receive in our childhood to who and what we may be? He describes this childhood calling as an 'annunciation' when we experience a sense of destiny in the path we may find ourselves following. We are literally stopped in our tracks by the sense of rightness in this calling before the mundane world with all its injunctions of what we should and should not do calls us away from this sense of bliss. And yet, all our lives, we are struggling to realize this script, this life calling. Each time our path pulls us inextricably towards it, we experience that sense of exhilaration mingled with a call to adventure. We lift our heads to sniff the pollen and taste the nectar on our lips. Without contact with that calling we become disconnected and as, Hillman cites 'I believe we have been robbed of our true biography – that destiny written into the acorn – and we go to therapy to recover it.'

Recently, due to the ongoing loss of honeybees, we are learning that their pollination alone is responsible for 20% of the food we eat, including coffee and tea. We take pollination for granted until it fails. In Japan because of the overuse of insecticides, the workers have to pollinate their almond blossom trees by hand. Imagine how long that takes! As overpopulation highlights food shortages that may touch our western countries, we are realizing our dependence on nature, not just for harnessing raw materials with which we clothe and make homes for ourselves, but also for our peace of mind and sanity. It is no coincidence that the original sanatoriums resided within an expanse of trees. Cross culturally nature has been the greatest inspiration for artists, poets, musicians and sculptures and not to mentions scientists. Newton's whole theory of gravity came as a result of an apple falling on his head. Spacecrafts are modeled on the flight of birds and today steel thread is being modeled on the components of spider's thread.

Our lack of awareness around our connectivity to nature is rooted in a paradigm that has been around for four hundred years. This paradigm of living within a mechanistic universe was conceived by Rene Descartes and Isaac Newton who, themselves, were theologians. Applying their mechanical laws to the living world brought nature under mankind's duress. As long as nature was regarded as inanimate and mechanical, an 'I and it' relationship existed between man and nature, rather than an 'I and Thou' as conceived by Martin Buber. 'I and Thou' includes the soul, whereas 'I and it' precludes it. Regardless of this old paradigm we are still embedded in the matrix of nature. After all, paradigms come and go as human civilization rises and falls. But nature is constant; she was here long before we came and will continue long after us. Our viewpoint of nature is tragically flawed until, like our ancestors, we can see the human race as part of its living matrix. The belief that there is the world of humanity and the world of nature, which is every other living being, is how we are ultimately crucifying ourselves. Within this paradigm exists an uncomfortable divide between nature and machine. Since, as Ken Wilber reveals in his writings, consciousness evolves by including the old, rather than splitting off from the past, this 'us' and 'them' way of being only impedes progress rather than facilitating it. We can only move forward by building a bridge between the old and the new. Really, these divisions exist within each one of us and because we are not able to deal with this, we relegate our inner opponent to the unconscious and make it conscious by projecting it onto the 'other'. Although we may not be able to understand the opposition, we can at least open to the fact that this was right for the time, or that political belief is right for that person given their background. This is not giving in, or excessive pluralism. This is tolerance.

Joseph Campbell, one of the greatest mythologists of our time, said shortly before he died that our old myths were dying and were being supplanted by new ones. A new paradigm is emerging and like the 'hundredth monkey syndrome', more and more people are countering the divisions by bridge building between science and nature. These bridge builders are scientists and thinkers like Rupert Sheldrake, David Bohm, Ervin Lazlo,

Edward Wilson and Matthew Fox. By their insights, they have made the new emerging paradigm conscious; that we are all inter-connected. In the context of this new paradigm; as beings intimately connected to nature, we are subject to the same process of evolution. Embedded in the matrix of nature we experience this field of energy psychologically and spiritually. In other words, on a psychospiritual level we are cyclically called back to the *Long Wait* as part of our collective developmental process. Whether we are conscious of this or not has a profound effect on our well being. Bringing consciousness to this is not something that can be grasped purely on a mental level, so it is not necessarily a question of intelligence, or even spiritual awareness. It is both experiential and phenomenological. And by this I mean accessed through the inner and outer senses. A child who lives very much in a phenomenological world can grasp it quickly. We adults, because of the accumulated debris of our mindsets, have to work a little harder at letting go and allowing this field to seep into us through our senses. This 'seeping through' can happen on holiday, or when we are relaxed or walking the dog. It is probably more likely to happen while directly in contact with nature, through a walk, open window or looking at flowers in a vase than through meditation. This is because many of us have too many mindsets around what meditation should be and should not be to access that phenomenological activity. A guided meditation or visualization exercise could be useful here.

Whether we can access this awareness of being embedded in nature's matrix or not does not really matter. We still have to bear the *Long Wait*, whether we experience this as a calling or a term of imposed limitation or not. It is just that entering the phenomenological field makes the *Long Wait* more bearable, because there is meaning and purpose in the process. Suffering on a spiritual or psychological level without meaning can be debilitating and depressing. Without finding meaning in suffering we refer to an event as 'senseless', which means without feeling or life. Through meaning we are able to access purpose and vision which bring us in direct alignment with the Self, the highest we can express while living in the world of matter. When in alignment with Self, we find a strength, vision and purpose beyond our own. We access the strength to bear our condition because we know that the condition, whatever it is, is not *all* of us.

Psychiatrist, Viktor Frankl, who spent many years during the wartime in a Nazi death camp, wrote about this in his book, *Man's Search for Meaning*. Amidst existing and working in intolerable subzero and near to starvation conditions, he found that prisoners who could find meaning in their suffering through realizing that life was giving them unique circumstances to strengthen them, bore their condition with dignity. Founded on this resolve, nothing appeared to take away their dignity. They had made an inner commitment to a purpose which was to be their lifeline. Viktor Frankl talked to his fellow prisoners about this, saying that it would be easier if they had a spiritual connection, but not impossible without as long as the connection existed within something outside and beyond the death camp. He noticed the prisoners that lived in the past or in a mental dream world, went to pieces earlier and did not survive long. They gave up purpose and vision. He said the key was in changing from demanding *why* this was happening to them, to: *what* was life asking of them? This method is used as a valuable tool in cognitive therapy and is referred to as 'reframing'.

Known Waiting

Let's look at the *Long Wait* and see why it is so difficult to bear without having resource to meaning. Waiting seems interminable and intolerable when we do not know *if* and *when* it will end. Comments like, 'It will pass' can offer empathy, but nothing concrete. We live in a world of parameters embedded within time structures we can understand and come to terms with.

Pregnancy is 9 months. In England, children go to school at 5, enter secondary school round about 11 and go to college or work at 18. We work until we are 65 and within that time frame we will probably take out a mortgage which will be paid off in so many years. From an early age we are saving up for a pension, taking out life insurance and working on building safe ground through an assortment of health protection schemes, immunizations, drugs, support networks, promotions that will enable us to continually upgrade our life. Our systems of waiting have both context and meaning. We wait for promotion. Wait to marry and have children and wait for our holidays and breaks. Most of us know what we are waiting for. This is *known* waiting. Known waiting is moderately comfortable, aside from the usual impatience and frustration which precede realizing that goal. Knowing the goal and the journey takes away a lot of the anxiety.

Transformative Waiting

Transformative waiting is without cultural parameters and, therefore, is largely unknown. Being in the unknown touches on deep existential issues about life and death, meaning and purpose. Because we are living in the unknown, the time spent in this process may seem interminable; each hour experienced as a lifetime. Transformative waiting leads into the *Wilderness* experience, because we have to dig deeper to make sense of our experience; to get in touch with our Source, whatever form that may take. Transformative waiting takes us beyond our known experience and by constraining us in limitation actually catapults us beyond our limits. Transformative waiting creates the chrysalis, or bud, in which everything we need to know in the future is held, releasing itself when *our time has come.*

Let us look at transformative waiting, which can take place on either a physical, mental, emotional or spiritual level. Most of the conditions impact on several levels simultaneously. Examples of these may be:

Grief after the loss of a loved one or a job.

Waiting for a medical prognosis for yourself, relative or close friend. (I have found while working in a hospital that most people would rather know that they have some serious condition, than be left not knowing anything.)

Waiting for bed space to come up so that a life saving operation can take place. .

Waiting for a missing child to turn up.

Waiting for a loved one with an incurable illness to die.

Waiting to emerge from depression that can take anything from a couple of weeks to a year or so.

Waiting for a mortgage or loan to be granted.

Waiting for someone to be cleared of a crime they did not commit.

Waiting for a reaction or response to something that has taken a great deal of courage to express or that you regret doing.

Spiritually, it can be waiting for lost spiritual connection to return.

On a smaller scale waiting for an important train that has been delayed.

Awaiting exam results.

Awaiting the results of a pregnancy test.

Waiting for our lives to open up.

Whatever the form transformative waiting takes, it involves a sustained period of anxiety, sometimes sadness, frustration and helplessness. Sometimes, and this is important, the *Long Wait* may not have a form, although seemingly unrelated events may have preceded its onset. This is not unusual, so may be experienced as depression. Sometimes the form can only become visible when it is conscious. Even if you know a little about the form, most of the ground around the *Long Wait* remains in the unconscious. Within this debilitating medium of powerlessness, we struggle to make sense of the situation in whatever way we can. And the meaning and strength we find may bring us onto ground we may not have traveled before; like seeking the help of an alternative practitioner, spiritual teacher, healer or a support group. We reach out to something greater than ourselves, taking us again into unknown territory, but also where there is a map to follow, guidance to offer.

Signs and Symptoms of the Long Wait

Reach into your body, into the tension and see if there is a symbol your body may offer you. Try not to be too judgmental when you perceive the symbol. Everything you experience is relevant at this time. You may be given an empty vase or a flower or an egg. Whatever the symbol, explore it thoroughly. Turn it over so that you can look at it from different angles. Does it smell? What color is it? What is its texture? Even if it seems boring and uninteresting, do not disregard it. See what it has to offer you, has it a story to tell? What does it evoke in you emotionally? Does it belong to the past? It may be useful to make a sketch of it or a painting.

Because the symptoms we are experiencing may seem trivial or uncomfortable,we can push them down in an effort to get rid of them. But in this type of soul work, everything has a story and is of value. Because we tend to censor everything on a mental level, we denigrate what is important and informative. Those of us who identify more with our feelings, may be just as guilty of not paying attention to what our senses are trying to tell us by blocking them out by overeating, oversleeping or engaging in incessant activity.

Underneath these are recognizable symptoms of the *Long Wait*:

Mental and physical stuckness

Low self-esteem

Anxiety

Feelings of dread

Vivid dreams, often about death; water and ocean dreams or dark places
Suicidal thoughts
Feelings of regression; going back to the past in thoughts and dreamlife.

Waiting in Hope

Life is the event that we are in the midst of, yet most of us would consider ourselves to be in a state of waiting. As John Lennon wrote; 'Life happens while we're busy making other plans.' Yet, how long have we been waiting for this life event?

Some of us even know what we are waiting for; like the right job; the right partner; exam results; a new car or the weather to change. The rest of us find our state of waiting more indefinite. We may be living in hope that our circumstances will change; that we will get better, that some member of our family who is causing us great concern, is going to change or die even! If 'hope' was a geographical place in the world, it would be overpopulated. So many people would want to live there! In a sense, many of us are waiting for a miracle. And, although miracles *do* happen, they usually happen when we are not expecting them!

Waiting in hope, if it is vague and goes on indefinitely, can easily give rise to a sense of helplessness and defeat. This is because we are *waiting* rather than *living*. No wonder we feel drained and have no energy! Energy goes to life, to being, not to waiting – at least the waiting that is based on hopes and vague dreams rather than transformative waiting which possesses its own goal and purpose. In the latter, there usually is no choice on the personality level. In dreamy hopeful waiting it can be a way of escaping the commitment that has to be made to life. Too often, underlying the hope, there is a desire to be rescued by something or someone. Hope can be very passive where we can cling to the thought that one day things will be better, if we do not make any effort to change our situation. I think this is what the poet, T.S.Eliot, tried to convey in the *Four Quartets,* quoted at the beginning of this chapter.

Having faith that the Divine in whatever form it manifests will come to meet us is proactive; setting into motion forces that will support and aid us in our chosen journey. If we are serious about our intention to take this journey, we have to act 'as if' to make any progress.

There is a fundamental law that applies to change. And that is, events cannot change unless we *accept* them first; accept our present circumstances and ask ourselves the question which we never seem to ask. The question Lancelot should have asked the Fisher King; 'Who does the grail serve?' And the question we need to ask is a magical, transformative one too: *What is this experience teaching me? What is it in service of?*

I had a couple of friends who worked as counselors in a prison and were involved with the Prison Ashram Project. They lent me a book called *We're All Doing Time.* It was a very insightful book written by an ex-prisoner for other prisoners, yet more and more people on the 'outside' found they could relate to it too. Hardly surprising, since we live in a world of matter and by our attitudes and life lessons we are all prisoners to circumstances, relationships, desires, possessions, health, many of which we believe give us a sense of security.

The truth of it is that we are all doing time. You, me, the family next door, the dog, the cat, the tree that has stood at the end of the driveway since we moved in, all of us are here for a period of years, some longer, others shorter and we are invited to learn within that framework. Ironically, the time when we gather the majority of our learning material is during the waiting periods, in between the activities. If we regard the waiting as useless and valueless, we are throwing away the richness of life. We are throwing away the manure. We are undervaluing the whole life process. And because we are part of life, we ultimately undervalue ourselves, each other. How often do we judge ourselves and each other by the amount of things we are 'doing' and achieving?

In prison, 'doing time' is known as a life sentence and regarded as a punishment. I would prefer to call it a learning experience because that is exactly what it is. In prison the inmates are usually kept busy, there is an active routine to the day. There are opportunities to learn valuable lessons about relationships with others in a small institution where everything is magnified and there is no escape. Having been to boarding school myself, I have some understanding of this; where day and night you are living in close proximity with others and working within an institutional structure where rules have to be respected and adhered to. Rules, rather than being negative, are natural boundaries, which to a greater or lesser extent, can be persuaded to bend or may buckle under pressure and consequently change. Rules like routine become rituals to live by. They wield a framework of purpose into a life. However challenging our daily routine, we can always make conditions more harmonious by aligning the rules we live by with our soul's purpose; for that is where the real importance lies. It is by living in conscious relationship with our soul's purpose that a sense of freedom begins to form.

Because we are not in a so-called prison or institution, we regard ourselves as 'free'. But I have found, as I am sure many of you have, that the greatest sense of imprisonment can be caused by internal conflicts rather than any tangible material condition. A change of perspective can completely free us. Within ourselves, we can feel just as restricted and socially cut off as a prisoner in an isolation block. Many of us have psychological conditions which imprison us, like agoraphobia, social phobia or claustrophobia. Some of us have illnesses or feel imprisoned by our family, our job, our money or lack of it, our home. And even if we have all the trappings which society says gives us freedom, including having a couple of pension funds, we still feel imprisoned. In our continual effort to lose ourselves and establish a greater freedom, we are actually tightening the 'chains' which bind us.

Moving beyond the traps of blame, accusation, condemnation, anger and frustration is where magic and healing take place. This is because we are no longer held in bondage by corrective injunctions which kept us safe when we were children, but have become guided by an inner sense of rightness instead. Rightness emerges from an awakening of conscience. We have accepted the situation and asked the question which will transmute the base metal of our grueling circumstances into wisdom and enlightenment. Questions expand consciousness, moving it from a personal and emotional level to a mental level and ultimately a spiritual one.

Always ask questions. Endeavor to be open and curious; for this is food for the inner child. As Walt Whitman expressed in his wonderful poem, *Song of Man* 'Question all that you have learned. Dismiss all that offends the soul.'

As children we always asked questions, but as we grow older, we ask less and less in order to fit into the world and not be seen as ignorant. Because of that, a large part of us closes down and becomes unconscious.

Staying in the Process

Waiting can be anticipatory when waiting for the days to get lighter and longer or the birth of a baby. The urgency of need and excitement seem to push the awaited event even further away, so that an hour can seem like an eternity. We know this, so we try to focus on other things, filling our life with activity in the hope that busyness will alleviate uncomfortable feelings of frustration, impatience and powerlessness. It is because we cannot move any more in a direction or because we have had to defer further action to realize something, that we pour the trapped energy into activity, in order to make our lives more manageable. There is nothing wrong with activity as long as it does not render us unconscious to our inner spiritual and psychological life. Activity for its own sake can be both numbing and addictive. And yet our culture supports constant activity and working, and in our relationships with others we confirm our cultural roots by saying we have to work more 'because we need the money', or because we want to either get as much out of life as possible, or give as much as we can because there is so much need around us.

Waiting is hard, and despite innumerable opportunities in life to perfect our approach to this, we never seem to get any better at it. This is because we perceive the waiting process to be a wholly negative situation. And this too is because we do not intuit the process; both its necessity and purpose. If we understand the process, we can accept it as normal and structure our life round it. We can even begin to welcome it for the wisdom it can offer us.

Through the lens of the world, waiting is seen as a waste of time, an idling away of life, a point at which we encounter an obstacle so great that it thoroughly impedes our progress. Yet there are periods of waiting in life which, because we understand the process, we see as quite natural. Because we understand the purpose of pregnancy we make room for it and prepare for the event. We can approach this with happiness, excitement and anticipation.

When we can begin to understand that each waiting process is a type of pregnancy, taking place on either a mental, physical, emotional and spiritual level, we can accept it more readily. Ironically, someone who is critically ill and 'waiting' to die, is experiencing a form of pregnancy. The patient is preparing to leave the world of form as we know it, while those left behind are already conceiving a new life which is born from the personal loss. Pregnancy is a time of adjustment, of ripening, involving gestation and incubation. It is also a time of letting go, of death even to an old way of life.

Again our lack of insight to these internal processes are a reflection of the material world we live in where outward events become more important than the waiting period; where activity and progress is seen positively and breaking down and entropy as negative. Death and birth follow each other like the black and white squares on a chessboard, and the waiting process is the bridge, the transition point where we move between the two.

I have applied this technique to my own experience and found that it works, really works. It took a long time for me to understand or apply this technique, because humility has not been my best quality!

Although many of us can accept that we spend a lot of time waiting instead of living or being, the sort of waiting I am concerned with here is the *Long Wait* which precedes the birth of a new event and follows a period of loss, surrender, sacrifice and death. On a world level we are in the midst of the 'credit crunch' where resources have been stretched to their limit because of corporate greed. No work is in isolation because it impacts on all levels. Just as the humble earthworm's task of breaking down the soil is crucial to the smooth functioning of the ecosystem, people in positions of monetary power can disregard the workers who tend the business at the bottom level. We have to learn that we cannot go back to the old model of exploiting every opportunity for more and more. Instead we need to downsize and create a new infrastructure which enfolds all and exiles none. We are all dependent on each other, whether we are capable of grasping this or not. As a result of this corporate greed in the western world, there is mass unemployment which has a knock on effect on the property market where houses are being repossessed and we have to make do with what we have rather than the instant throw-away culture that has predominated so long. We have to plant different seeds and tend their growth, nurture them through the difficult times so that we can create a holistic way of living and being. We are invited to go back in order to go forward.

The *Long Wait*, although it can manifest externally, takes place inwardly; within the crucible of the soul after it has been fired by the emotions and cooled in the mind. To fully understand the nature of the *Long Wait* we need to use the tree to illustrate this.

Picture a magnificent tree heavy with fruit. Then imagine the fruit falling, the leaves turning color, then scattering until the tree is stripped and naked. The days become colder and the winds are hash and unforgiving; tearing away at the branches, buffeting the trunk. Next, comes the snow, clothing the tree in a cold ethereal beauty, then the winds again. The dark mornings, the dark nights....

Although the tree looks dead in its stripped skeletal state, we know that it is not dead. This is because we have insight into the tree's continuity. We know it has been through this before. We know that if we examine the branches, we will see that there are buds on the twigs and that the tree will emerge in miraculous green glory in the spring. It just looks dead. We think nothing of it. We do not say; 'I wonder what's happened to that tree? It doesn't look very good. I wonder why it's not in leaf, or producing blossom or fruit?'

In fact, that would be ridiculous, until we remember that we make these demands of ourselves and each other!

Bifocal Vision

If we are not active and producing 'fruit', we feel depressed because we think something is wrong. We might go to the doctor, a therapist or a psychiatrist, because we have lost touch with our inner therapist who, if we consult it, will know exactly what is wrong and advise us accordingly. A good therapist who is aware of our soul's journey and therefore embraces the spiritual aspect of our self as well as the psychological one, will use what in psychosynthesis is called 'bifocal vision'. This is a way of looking at what is happening in the *foreground*, our presenting problem.

For example, in this case we will be feeling lonely and cut off from the world. And then they will look towards your Self to explore what is endeavoring to emerge in the *background*. By aligning to the Self, the therapist comes into contact with what is known as the 'emerging purpose'. At first the background may be invisible, inarticulate and insubstantial, but as it is coaxed into visibility by inclusion and acceptance, it becomes obvious that the soul is attempting to journey deeper into life experience. They will perhaps reframe our experience by acknowledging that although we are lonely and cut off from the world on a secular level, our soul is endeavoring to access a level of wisdom and insight which will be in service of the development of our life skills, and ultimately be of service to others.

We never grow or learn for our sake only; what we learn is assimilated on a world level too, through what Jung called the Collective Unconscious. Bifocally, our withdrawal from the world is part of a larger gestation experience which will be borne in consciousness when the time is ready.

Working Bifocally

The following exercise can be carried out with a partner; where the act of identifying the problem with an external mirror can enhance the exercise.

Close your eyes for a few moments and breathe slowly, allowing a little time to get in touch with the sensations in your body and your feelings.

Take an issue that is occupying you at the moment and write down a few details about it. Let go of these details and relax your senses and mind. Be aware of any images that are waiting to be recognized in the wings. Imagery is a natural way of making contact with the Self. Imagery bypasses the rational mind and communicates with that deeper part of the self. Make a note of what comes to light. Be aware of what happens to your body as you focus on the contents.

Again, close your eyes and take a little time to dis-identify from your feelings around this issue and the tension in your body.

Usually, contact with the Self will evoke a feeling of expansion, peace and a sense of rightness. Rather than feeling the need to flee from the body, which can be habitual when in the midst of change and crises, there is a growing sense of peace. As you work with this exercise more and begin to trust what you are picking up on a somatic and soul level, you will become more adept at recognizing the differences between both foreground and background, somatic level and soul level.

Because we scarcely understand this cyclical process in our own lives, we have only a dim appreciation of it happening in the lives of people around us. In fact, witnessing what is happening to other people both in our lives and through the global media in the light of breakdown and breakup, can be deeply unsettling. It is easy to make these unsettling people into objects of personal projection which intensify our 'shadow' and estranges us further. Deep down, if we do not accept these processes as natural and part of the rich complexity of human and soul development, we may dread it happening to us and close down to deeper processes within our psyche that can prepare us for difficulty in the future. This is why people who are experiencing a breakdown in relationship, health or communication, suddenly find all their friends have migrated. No one wants to know them when they are struggling. Some may not even return after the difficult time, but new and lasting contacts will emerge from the old; ones that empathize and lend insight to the experience rather than running away.

Because our inner process is unique to us, it may not synchronize with events that are going on around us or happening to our friends and family. It is easy to feel alienated and collapse into a desperate need to be accepted, loved and to fit in. This may take the form of increased activity, restlessness or destructive relationships based on sex or emotional blackmail. Just because a process or event is uncomfortable, it does not mean that it is wrong. Discomfort may be the very factor that causes us to make necessary changes.

A good therapist will be able to understand that we are in the midst of a life change and see that, like the stripped tree, we already have buds for the next stage of manifestation. They will encourage us to be less impatient and suggest things that we should do to help ourselves. Sometimes we may be at a complete standstill, unable to move anywhere. A therapist will support us in that; using bifocal vision to look beyond the standstill to see what is happening in the background, what is waiting in the wings.

We are now about to pass through another phase in our journey, that of feeling lost and unable to fix our situation in the ways we have known before. The wilderness can be stormy and challenging in that it does not seem to conform to anything we have known before….. but we are, although we dare not believe it, about to discover the 'still point'. That part that all mystics and hermits have had to pass through in order to access their wisdom. Allow yourself to not know, to be without direction or anchor. Surrender to that great Love that is not outside you, but within you…

Chapter 11

The Long Wait and the Wilderness

Although the *Wilderness* is encapsulated in the *Long Wait*, I have chosen to address it as a separate chapter. It involves a deepening and descent and is the gift that is waiting within this process. Gift, because it births insights that we can rarely find without descent. This is the wild card of the *Long Wait*. It is the initiatory passage into soul-making and the deeper mysteries.

Without guidelines to follow or some understanding of what is going on, the *Long Wait* can be a frustrating, grueling, even a frightening experience. Generally, there is a point of choice within the *Long Wait* when the soul makes a decision to enter more deeply into the experience and will often seek guidance through spiritual and emotional counseling or healing. This choice is not so much a conscious choice made on the level of the personality, but rather a surrendering of what is happening to something greater. In a sense, it is as if there is no choice, as if there is something destined about this process. And yet with this inner choice comes a peace bringing with it a sense of rightness. As if to affirm this decision, life events seem to conspire in making it all the more possible. A relationship that had reached an impasse ends; children leave home, our partner goes away on business or the firm one is working for has to cut back on staff so that voluntary redundancy is offered. If possible, it is advisable to take time out from work or the normal ritual of day to day

131

living for this process to take place. If the personality is uncon-scious to the needs of the soul or chooses to ignore the symptoms it is experiencing such as confusion, loss of purpose and meaning, it seems as if one is receiving a crash course in meeting with locked doors. Fighting against the soul's impulse to journey deeper, will only exacerbate the discomfort and suffering which may plunge us into physical or mental dis-ease. The resulting symptoms are the soul's way of communicating with us.

It is as if we find ourselves swimming endlessly against the tide and each time we make a concerted effort to break away, we find ourselves caught up in disturbing currents of our own making which threaten to drag us down to deeper levels of disil-lusionment and despair. The only way forward is through *surrender*, which is also the way of Grace. Grace *always* enters in where there is sacrifice and surrender because the heart is opened. Alternatively, there may be little conscious choice in this; where perhaps a great sacrifice is made by caring for a sick or terminally ill relative, or having to undergo a long period of personal illness or unemployment where there may be a sense of life having been closed down, together with a deep sense of imprisonment without any relief in sight.

It is as if we have been exiled from life. Yet...

What may be experienced as limitation and exile in the secular world, will hold the potential for expansion and healing in the inner world. The process is no different to the one that shapes the cycle of the tree; stripping off of leaves that are no longer needed to make way for a new cycle of bud, blossom and fruit.

In order to fully benefit from the *Wilderness* we need to change our outlook and understand that there is a gift waiting for us in this experience. Our soul is being offered training in order to grow in a new direction. Accepting the situation is the most positive step we can make and by this very act of acceptance we are changing the conditions around us. To be willing to work *with* the wilderness experience brings us the energy and support we need. Help and direction will come and we will experience a growing inner peace. And remember the importance of this: *The wilderness experience would not come to you unless you had the strength and capacity to go through with it.*

Remember this too: Your soul has invited these conditions into your life for your greater growth.

It is imperative that the wilderness experience is not viewed in a wholly pessimistic light, although the secular language of the world may enforce this belief; where loss and unemployment are interpreted in their most dire sense, rather than a transformative one. The *Long Wait* is a vital part of inner growth and the time in the wilderness is an *opportunity*, not a punishment. It is often during the *Long Wait* and the *Wilderness* that one's inner life may be totally transformed by changing spiritual and emotional beliefs and where new, stronger foundations are set amidst the crumbling old ones. Consequently, as inner affects outer, the life pattern will alter the life direction towards one of soul-making and purpose. Material values will drop into the background as new more substantial values emerge.

Basically, *Wilderness* is about nourishment. As we are shedding the world daily, we are gaining weight on a soul level. It is not surprising that during this period, people will often lose a lot of weight on a physical level as sustenance is being gained on other levels of being.

Although the *Wilderness* may be a period of exile from the material world, another door opens, one which welcomes us and whose values are based on rules and laws we may not be familiar with. 'Teachers' will come to us in real life or on an inner level who will guide us through this period. These real life teachers may take the place of our friends who are either never around when we need them or, more commonly, we can no longer relate to them. They may not fit into our mindset of what a teacher should be. They may be 'oddballs' themselves who live on the fringes of society, but if we are honest, then we will seek their company rather than the company of those outside our internal experience. Our teachers may be animals or, as in my case, can be in the form of the natural environment. Nature ultimately is the greatest teacher of all and her lack of judgment and unquestioning acceptance of us however we are is comforting.

What is the Wilderness?

Throughout history, the wilderness has been a place where disciples from varying religious backgrounds have made a pilgrimage to seek spiritual guidance or contact with their ancestors. For the Aborigines it was their 'dreamtime' and for the shaman it was where he made contact with animal spirits. For the Buddhist monks it was a place set aside from the world. In the third century it was common for Celtic Christian monks to enter the desert to gain a closer contact with God. This was modeled on the Egyptian monks who would spend months even years in the desert seeking spiritual sustenance. These were the original Desert Fathers who followed St Paul's example of living in the desert, although I feel it is relevant to add here that there have been a number of women who spent time in the desert, several with periods of up to ten years. So perhaps these were the 'desert mothers'. Records abound throughout the centuries of hermits and hermitages existing all over the world for disciples of different religions.

In the British Isles such places existed on islands off the Hebrides where it was only possible for boats to come in to land a few months of the year, and I am thinking particularly of Iona where Columba meditated in a hermit's cell set within a circle of weathered rock. Bardsey Island was once known as the Isle of a Thousand Saints. Also there were hermits living on other remote places like the moors and throughout Wales. Unlike the much respected Upanishads in India who spent time withdrawing into the forest, in many Western Cultures hermits, anchorites and recluses have been regarded as oddballs rather than valued for their wisdom. Sadly, this reveals our own ignorance and inability to accept the value of solitude so sought after, yet feared in our modern society.

On Mount Athos in Greece, the monks would spend years in cells living in the wilderness within the confines of the island. It is interesting that the word 'hermit' derives from the Greek word, 'eremites', which means 'dwellers in the desert'. So the wilderness was and is a place of exile from the secular world. The biblical recording of Christ's time in the desert was 40 days which was more likely to have been 40 weeks, the period of human pregnancy. The *Long Wait*, as mentioned before, is a form of pregnancy.

Today, spiritual teachers like White Eagle, inform us that we are called to go through these periods of withdrawal in the midst of our daily life. The time of retiring for months in monasteries and convents is over for many of us who are spiritually conscious. We have entered a new turn of the spiral, finding peace within the busyness of everyday life. This is deeply challenging, yet undeniably strengthening, we are called to live that age old maxim of 'being in the world, but not of it'.

Sadly, and on an ecological level, all but one or two wildernesses have survived amidst our ever expanding culture, where development leads us further away from nature and consequently the inner processes taking place within us. Africa hangs on grimly to its last natural wilderness, while conservationists fight to keep this from the hungry modern day wolves. Our destruction of the wilderness is a rich metaphor for our alienation from nature and from that 'still place' within us. As we destroy the wild places outside, we also shut down to those wildernesses within, driving us further from realizing or understanding the gifts they can offer us; namely transformation and enlightenment. And yet by our excessive compulsion to make money out of every living tree, we are creating an ever encroaching wasteland which parallels our growing sense of spiritual impoverishment.

Why we Keep Ourselves Busy

One of the most profoundly debilitating conditions in our Western world is the experience of emptiness. In fact our deep existential fear around this feeds into and sustains our culture of busyness. Busyness itself has almost become a God and those of us who choose to worship at this altar, receive kudos of respect, admiration and are seen as a shining example to the rest. This culture of busyness has grown to such immense proportions that we feel guilty if we are not busy or *doing* something, even if we know deep down that it is perfectly sane to take time out and breathe in. The tide of busyness rolls into our lives each day in the form of the media, our friends and relations and we find ourselves sucked in, whether we like it or not. In fact, it takes tremendous resolve and inner strength not to get sucked in and find ourselves muttering the mantra for today, 'I'm too busy'. or 'I haven't got time.' An example of this was shown on the news several years ago; where a Buddhist group in Manchester were offering meditative practice as a way of coping with the stress of Christmas shopping. There was an opportunity to take a little time out and receive instruction on meditation and the oppor-tunity to feed the innermost self's desire for nourishment. One woman being interviewed when asked whether she thought this was a good idea, threw up her hands in dismay, saying. 'I haven't got time.'

But how do we get to be so busy? And, more to the point, why?

Most 'busy' people, including ourselves perhaps, will stead-fastly agree that we cannot help it. Busyness happens to us. It's not something we have much control over. The world imposes itself upon us. We also need to earn a living. You cannot earn a living if you are not busy and do not work. And yet people who have retired exclaim that they are just as busy as they were when they were working. Which proves that busyness has very little to do with earning a living. But, we may argue, there are so many things that need doing in the world. So many people need our help? And this may be true. But if everyone is so busy with doing, then who is actually being? After a little hesitation the argument will continue, 'People haven't got time *to be* these days. Being is a thing of the past.'

I would suggest two things here and then look at them individually.

The first is that busyness is not the same as work, although busyness may become a form of work itself. The second is to return to emptiness and our fear of it and the suggestion that we keep ourselves busy to keep emptiness at bay.

One of the fundamental keys in unlocking this dilemma is to look at choice and will. Since we define ourselves and affirm our level of autonomy by the choices we make; the way we respond to life is crucially important. Choice is one of the first things the young child learns in order to direct and exert his will. He learns to say 'no' and realizes the immense power in this over his personal environment. The sooner he learns the power of choice, the sooner he gets to exert his will. The well known tantrums throughout childhood are due to the child having his will thwarted by his parents or other caretakers. Later, as a teenager and young adult, his will comes to the fore again as he uses it to define his personality but also to separate from his parents who have held his will in check through strong injunctions which define what is right and what is wrong. This imposed definition of what is right and wrong within the climate of family, culture and society will continue to exert their influence in the form of superego injunctions in adult life. This is until the adult is able to make his own individual decisions on right and wrong.

As will is fundamental to our sense of personal power, choice is the servant of will. Yet, at some point, we choose to not make conscious choices over our life. Instead we allow ourselves to become swept up in the tide of life in order to block out that part of us that craves for stillness and rest. I remember when I first became conscious of what I was doing when I was working in a nursing home where the work was often relentlessly heavy, so that staff became sick themselves and extra help was needed. For the second time that week I had been called in on my day off and remember thinking, 'Why not? I don't have to think and be with myself if I go in.' This has repeated itself often with fellow colleagues in the hospital who have been called in on their day off and I have heard similar comments. 'Well — I don't know what else to do. I just get bored at home.' And this is not to say that there is not a strong pull to be of service in the caring work or that we may need the 'extra' money'. But that does not take away the first thought that stems from an inability to be alone with ourselves for any length of time. When we give up personal choice, we go unconscious to that part of ourselves and in that become part of an unspoken rule in our culture. This is referred to as 'consensus reality.' Charles Tart, a psychologist and psychiatrist refers to this unspoken collective agreement as the 'consensus trance'. And this is not to say that we do not have personal will or choice. We do, but in limited areas. Really the 'consensus trance' is one of survival and underscores how we go unconscious to parts of ourselves that , if conscious, may force us to make uncomfortable choices and changes in our lives.

Because of our deep need to 'belong' in society and not be alienated by our beliefs, we keep each other in this trance, by admonishing what we see as threatening in each other and reinforce what keeps us unconscious. These unconscious networks are very hard to break because their roots are tribal and ancient. It is through this unconscious tribal network that we maintain old paradigms, and through the breaking down of this network that we begin the challenging task of creating new paradigms.

The reason why I am writing this and echoing the work of

other innovative writers, psychologists and philosophers before me and the reason you are reading this now is because as a culture we are beginning to emerge from this consensus trance. In fact, we are in psychological terms, 'individuating', finding our collective and personal autonomy again. Like the 'hundredth monkey syndrome' who washes his potato in seawater because the taste of salt gives it a better flavor. By our example, we are having an impact on the field of consciousness. We do not even have to convert anyone, impact occurs on a more subtle level.

Work is a daily necessity whether we work in the conventional sense or not. We all have our daily work, our daily routine which gives us structure, meaning and purpose. For some, who are more fortunate in their choice of work, this may be a vocation, a source of inspiration to themselves and the rest of the world. For others, the work although menial and repetitive, may be a way of feeding their family and provide meaning this way or it may finance another vocation that lies closer to the heart, like an artistic calling or running an animal shelter. This work is a necessity on a financial and value level. Day to day menial work disciplines the body and mind, but creating meaning from this engages the heart and soul.

The Quality of Being

So what did these religious aesthetics do in the desert? we ask ourselves, for whom the thought of a day or week alone in the desert or wilderness conjures up horror and disbelief.

In our everyday world where the emphasis is on 'doing', we have lost sight and sense of what it is 'to be', just as we no longer appreciate the differences between doing and being; both of which should exist in equal quantities in our life. In fact it is the very act of being that gives our life quality. Quality time is being, breathing in, recharging. Being can be an active form of visualization like daydreaming. Meditation is a form of active being, so is prayer. Being does not use energy, it *generates* energy. People who can 'be' in their work and life, seem to achieve an enormous amount with the minimum of effort. Doing on its own is an effort. It is stress and strain. Being comes first and true doing arises out of being. Being is the boundless deep, like witnessing a beautiful landscape or piece of music. The inspiration that is derived from this experience becomes the energy of doing. Children know how to be; that is why they have so much natural energy. Being, in actuality, is a state of unconditional living; which completely contradicts the myth that you have to put something into life to get anything out. There is a sense of being enthused and enlivened by a source of supply rather than being driven and drained by goals that we can never seem to reach. Being is when we let go of expectations and yet, because of this a different sort of expectation comes to the fore, an expectation of the miraculous. In giving up material expectation we are actually allowing a greater or divine form of expectation to manifest, which is the Self. And it does.

I expect you remember when you had a day which just flowed, rather than snared on countless obstacles. Everything flows along smoothly and opportunities appear to literally fall into our lap. We find ourselves in the right place, talking to the right people and not only that, doing the right thing. We feel good about life, about ourselves. We are in harmony with ourselves. And yet we do not appear to have done anything! Yet, it has been a successful day, one in which we have achieved a greater sense of self and understanding of life. Doing without being is hard work. Being and doing flow together in twin rivers. And just being generates the will to express and all doing literally becomes and act of being.

Can you recall a time or day in your life when you were just being?
A time that flowed and you felt in harmony with your life?
Do you allow yourself time to just 'be' throughout the day?
Can you remember what you did? or did not do?
Do you allow yourself to be now in your life?

Back to the Wilderness...

From what I have read, the desert fathers prayed and meditated a lot. Many of them practiced a form of ceaseless prayer which covers all manner of worldly conditions; from people who had lost loved ones to those who were about to meet with an accident. I remember being very touched by this latter form of prayer; to think that someone somewhere is praying for unknown people who are in the midst of traffic accidents etc!

Perceiving this way of life through worldly eyes may seem a ponderous and monotonous task to undertake, until one begins to understand that in the desert and the wilderness time drops down to a natural rhythm and simultaneously the pressures that drive us so much in the secular world, fall away. There is a harmony in this natural rhythm which is healing for the body, mind and soul.

But what does the wilderness and desert mean to us today who live so much in the secular world and do not have the time or capacity to enter into such long periods of contemplation in a voluntary way?

The important thing to remember here is that we do not have to be a monk or a religious ascetic to enter the wilderness any more than we need to step outside our front door. This is because the monk, the spiritual ascetic are no longer outside us, they are inside us too.

The tree stands firm during the *Long Wait*, allowing the days to come and go. It does not go anywhere. It does not have to do anything but be and allow the cycle to move through and around it.

Many of us know that although we can be in the midst of a group of people, we can simultaneously feel alone. Similarly, we can be alone in nature or simply sit in a chair and yet we can experience a sense of union with all the elements of life, the landscape, humans, animals, the wind, the trees.

I mentioned at the beginning of this chapter that we often

have a choice whether to go deeper into our wilderness experience so that we can make preparations in our life. But in some cases, like my own, there seems to be little conscious choice, rather choice is made on a soul level.

I spent ten years within the wilderness without fully acknowledging what was happening. On the outer worldly level I was experiencing a long and intense depressive illness. I entered it at 21 and began to emerge in my early thirties. It was within this wilderness where I was physically, mentally and emotionally exiled from the material world, that I began my career as a writer and developed a deep and lifelong contact with nature. During this prolonged experience most of my activities took place on an internal level. I had visions, psychic experiences where I would spend time outside my body, visiting various levels of existence, and experiencing creative inspiration. Although I believed that my soul had made this choice, my personality often rebelled against this isolation. I desperately wanted to be living a 'normal' life doing the normal things that young people do.

Like any experience, my time in the wilderness had various phases. Although much of my experience was a general impression of being 'underground', I did have days where the light seemed to break through and I experienced a great sense of joy and union with that nameless divinity which we refer to as God. At these times I knew I was loved and cared for and the pain I was in was not intended as a penance, but rather as a learning experience. I would experience a heightened perception which would be exemplified in my creative work.

Most of the time, however, I felt in prison. It was nature who very often held the key to that prison. Days would pass where I would metaphorically 'sit at her feet' and learn about the seasons and her cycles. It was during that period that I made a pact with the trees that I would do whatever I could in my life to help them, for they had given me so much wisdom. Since then I have helped plant thousands of trees up and down the country. I have planted trees to celebrate events in my life and the lives of friends. I have planted trees for people, for causes, for hopes and dreams and only have to think of an area of trees that I helped plant and feel the connection with their environment.

I have since wondered why I experienced such an intense period of being in the wilderness, I can only conclude that, somewhere along the way, my soul must have chosen to do so in order to impart some of my experience to others and this makes sense since my work of running a spiritual magazine for seven years and editing books to fill a spiritual need, encouraged me to make use of my experience. Additionally, I have learned a lot about fear and how it can become a driving force in our lives, just as love can be. Fear comes from a general lack of trust in life, but it is also there to keep us safe during times in our life when we are not physically or psychically strong enough to exert our will in the world. The trick is in discriminating between neurotic fear and existential fear so that we can have the courage to move forward to find the strength and love that is waiting for us in that moment of daring. Neurotic fear is the debris of long held mindsets that we will fail or make a huge mistake if we do something. It is a symptom of the Self calling us to dare to make another step in life which takes us through the threshold of the known to the unknown. Every threshold is a minor initiation of death and rebirth. Existential fear is the fear of betraying our deeper Self. Moving forward in any way always brings up fear because we know that we will have to change. Also that change will mean that a part of us will die even if that death will be ultimately beneficial to us. The part that has to die is some perception we held of ourselves and the world which kept us from engaging in life more fully. Kept us imprisoned. More often than not, the death that we fear is psychological death.

Having lived out such a prolonged period of inner activity, I can honestly say that living a life on the inner level takes far more courage and strength to keep on than difficult circumstances in the outer world. Inner activities can be draining as they can be enriching and, consequently, I have a deep respect for all those encountering challenging inner experiences. It is not easy to forge on through difficulties that few people living in the material world can see, let alone acknowledge.

As children I believe we know intuitively which direction we will grow in. As children we have a wisdom and a perception that we quickly lose and seem to spend the rest of our lives trying to find again!

As a child my obsession with mythology and particularly Persephone and the Underworld was preparing my psyche for what I would encounter all through my twenties. I have covered much of this in my previous book, *Depression as a Spiritual Journey.*

Although our time in the *Wilderness* may compel us to make worldly sacrifices, it is not without its gifts; priceless ones because we cannot buy them or barter them. The gifts of clarity, insight and inner peace are ones which all men and women seek at some point in their lives, whether they find it through disappointments in the material world or through a more lonely and contemplative path. Wisdom is gained through *reflection, contemplation* and *aspiration*. Gifts which are essential to function as a multi-layered human being in this world. Without exploring any of these three states and allowing them to take root in our consciousness, we cannot develop into our full potential, we remain half asleep, muddling through our life and filling it with incessant activity in a effort to block out the unconscious. No wonder we are paranoid and so full of fear!

Exercise in Being
This simple exercise can be carried out several times a day and will help you to relax more and locate the source of what is driving you to achieve and do more.
Be aware of being today, rather than doing.

How does your body feel? Does it feel poised to spring onto the next event? If so, notice where the resistance is held in your body.
Are your hands and jaw clenched? Does guilt drive you to doing?
Think of something you enjoy along the lines of being which can be anything from painting, to daydreaming to baking a cake. When did you last carry out these activities? What blocks you from enjoying them?

Try to carry out at least two of the tasks below each day and add others that are relevant to you to the list. For some cycling, swimming or gentle jogging may hold a quality of being that relaxes the mind, rather than stresses it. I include a few more suggestions here, but you may have ones which are meaningful to you that you might like to add:
Relaxing in a bath
Taking a relaxing walk and noticing the world around you, without judging
Swimming noncompetitively
Gazing up at the stars
Painting a picture
Playing ball with your children or grandchildren
Reading a book
Planting seeds or bulbs
Day dreaming
Feeding the ducks at a local pond or lake
Making a collage of natural elements like leaves, seeds, grass, fur, tree bark (according to what is in season)
Sitting on a bench and watching the world go by
Having coffee with a friend or by yourself if preferred
Knitting or sewing
Listening to some calming music.
From this sample list it is clear that being is rarely a state of non activity, neither is it passive. Rather it is reflective, contemplative and evokes a sense of richness and quality.

We have finally entered the eye of the storm, the final cycle in the *Long Wait*. We have passed through the cyclone and are pivoted in the eye. Despite feelings of anxiety about the future, a sense of loss and disorientation, we are beginning to experience a peace. A 'peace that passeth all understanding'. In fact, the peace has always been there, but our wilderness experience has brought us closer to it. On the outer level, our lives may resemble a shipwreck or a forest that has been razed to the ground by strong chastening winds, but it no longer matters. In fact nothing matters … only that we are here now. Reflection is the first of the three strands of re-orientation before we emerge into another cycle. We now have time to reflect on all the events of our life that have led us to where we are now.

Chapter 12

First Quality of the Wilderness: Reflection

A gust of wind swept across the water, breaking up its surface into silver fragments. The tree shook, the bare branches moving restlessly. Little by little, a stillness came and the tree's reflection in the water became clear and still. A peace entered into the landscape. The same peace that underlay all creation, even the hurrying fretting steps of modern day life.

One of the greatest losses of this modern age is that of reflection. In the average day those of us caught up in the merry-go-round of life events lack any time for reflection. If we have a space in our day, we are challenged by the media to watch television, listen to the radio, chat on Facebook, 'tweet' on Twitter or become caught up in some other activity. Reflection is seen as an idle condition, or even an indulgence that few people feel they have the time to pursue.

Most of the people I have talked to feel they would like more time to reflect. And I know if I have not had the time or opportunity to reflect, I feel as if I am lacking a certain depth and quality to my life that makes me restless, unhappy and frustrated. It is often tempting to fill this existential vacuum with even more activity to alleviate the emptiness. It is also ironical that the more activity we become engaged in, the emptier we can feel. Overactivity creates a sense of inner impoverishment, whereas 'just being' is enriching as well as empowering.

To understand the whole concept of reflection and its meaning in our life we need to define what it is. The dictionary definition is 'meditative and thoughtful' or 'a turning or bending back on itself'. This latter definition clearly illustrates the process. When we reflect, we go back in time to recall events from the past. Images arise from the event which will bring us pleasure, nostalgia, love, fear, regret and anxiety. Because reflection occurs naturally, if we allow it space and time, it is vital to our understanding of past events. Reflection is how we make sense of events; it is a state of assimilation which allows us to integrate the past with the present. It can be part of a very important learning experience in that we can see by this process where we may have gone wrong in our relationships with people and the areas we need to work on in the future. Reflection is a synthesis of the past with the present. It is also a synthesis of heart, mind, spirit and soul. We are able to gain a clearer vision of ourselves. While the mind and body are caught up in the often frenetic activity of everyday life, we become cut off from our source like the trout returning to their homing ground to spawn new life. This results in an inner turbulence caused by conflicts we cannot resolve. We have lost our centre and, because of this state of inner disharmony, we become fragmented like the tree's reflection in the water in the wind...

But if we stop and cease from running, little by little a state of peace enters into our being and the inner fragmentation gives way to wholeness. Without this alignment with our centre and source we experience a sense of helplessness and powerlessness within. The world with all its distractions can only temporarily alleviate this and if we happen to find anyone with a modicum of wisdom, they will direct us back to our own front door or put us in touch with a spiritual development group.

Reflection in many ways has earned itself a lot of bad press and been associated with the negative term 'dwelling' on a situation; thus equating it with self-obsession and delusion. We say elderly people reflect a lot. And this is true because they have a whole lifetime to reflect on and, in a positive sense, draw strength from. In a sense the reflection is the 'interest' they have accumulated during the credit of their lifetime. Without interest we quickly use up a capitol. Similarly, without time for reflection we become exhausted and empty.

Reflection is not only positive, but keeps us sane. Without it, we become neurotic, stressed and unable to stop — literally. Over the last two decades, the speed of life has accelerated to such a degree that reflection and meditation are qualities which are easily sacrificed in our daily life for things we perceive are better, merely because they are activities. Many of us create activity for its own sake, not just because it is fashionable and socially acceptable but because we are afraid of its polarity, inactivity. Inactivity is a mirror where inner events come up for review. We are faced with ourselves, along with all our frustrations, needs, dreams and desires.

Without reflection we are hungry. More than that — we are starving! Eating food is one thing; but not having time to properly assimilate and digest that same food is tantamount to suffering from an anorexic condition.

Driven by inner hunger alone we race from one activity to another, looking, searching, and tasting without really digesting the food that we so desperately need. But these activities instead of assuaging us, just distract further, awakening even greater hungers, until we are almost driven to desperation with our own hunger; whatever that desperation may be; breakdown, neurosis, addiction or even suicide. No wonder we have eating disorders as our search for spiritual sustenance becomes embedded in physical food issues. We are hungry, starving even, but the panacea we seek is activated on the somatic level rather than the spiritual one.

Holidays which were originally 'holy days' and therefore

reflective in nature, have been transformed into ready made packages crammed full of activities that can make us feel like hamsters on tread wheels. Now, instead of feeling refreshed by a holiday, we invariably need time to recover. Where holidays or holy days marked a form of retreat from the secular material world, they have become an almost nightmarish descent into endless doing and becoming. Instead of shedding possessions and baggage we arm ourselves with enough possessions to crush any self-respecting mule. Instead of returning from our holy days spiritually enriched and mentally rested, we return with even more baggage, materially broke, emotionally scattered and spiritually impoverished. Reflection has no place in this whirlwind of distractions. Yet, thankfully, more and more people are realizing the need for rest in its truest sense and seeking retreat from the world.

Reflection is the stage which precedes the two other stages of aspiration and contemplation in the waiting period; these states that prevent us from sinking into a mental and emotional torpor and give our life meaning, substance and direction.

So let us look at reflection and the process which makes us so uneasy.

Because reflection requires time; a commodity we never feel we have enough of, we need to create this as the medium through which reflection will manifest. If we are to go for a walk in nature, or sit in the garden without any particular object in mind, thoughts will come up inside us. Thoughts that are usually connected with the past. We will think about earlier activities, meetings with people. Bits of conversation will repeat in our mind and maybe we will be charmed or haunted by some event. But at some point we will no longer feel as if we are observing the process that is going on inside us, we will find ourselves emotionally involved. Something – a sentence or an event will have triggered off a reaction in us and quite often we feel angry, irritable or frustrated. This is when we can feel uncomfortable because we sense we have lost control. We have moved from a state of quiet reflection to a smoldering obsession with an event or person.

Rather than run away from this and resume our hungry search for something to fill the gap inside us, we can remind ourselves that our feelings and emotions cannot change the past. The past is past. However, we can change the present by our reaction to it.

It is good to take a little time out to focus on our immediate surroundings, whatever they may be, and take a few deep breaths.

It is also important to remind ourselves that these emotional, often obsessive feelings, are part of a natural process. *Accept* them. They are part of our learning experience and are there to highlight something within us that needs working on, that we need to learn and understand — in order to let go of. The problem manifests when we cannot feel anything, or through denial do not allow ourselves to feel anything. That is when we lose our way and become unstuck, because we are emotional feeling beings. We need to be in touch with our feelings, to gain a greater understanding of ourselves. We cannot learn to rise above our feelings and emotions if we have no feelings or emotions to rise above! I have a counselor friend who has said many of the clients that come to her, don't know *what* to feel sometimes. They arrive in a state of unrest and are so out of touch with their feelings, that identifying any one particular emotion is not only a daunting task, but an impossible one too.

Similarly, introspection occurs when we become totally caught up and obsessed with something to such an extent, that we forget who we are and lose our centre. Remember our feelings and emotions cannot change an event or person, but they can affect our present.

Reflection, in a positive sense, brings us in touch with who we really are, what we are looking for and where we are heading. It is a lens through which we can glimpse a clear image of ourselves, a true reflection. Reflection is also a means through which insights can rise from the unconscious and break into the conscious mind, releasing fresh energy and inspiration. How often, while gardening or going for a country walk, do we find the answer to a seemingly insoluble problem or are able to see things in a new light? Ideally, reflection should become an integral part of our daily framework. And there are various tools which we can use to enable us to make optimum sense of our reflective abilities. These are: writing a letter; keeping a diary; knitting, gardening, walking or cycling in nature and swimming, preferably in the sea or natural water. These are activities that can be used as a catalyst through which reflection can work. An empty sheet of paper invites the unconscious to break into the conscious mind either though painting or writing. It is through creation and restful repetition that reflection manifests. When we create a part of ourselves, our life force enters into the work, whether it is a child, a piece of fabric or a letter and we animate what we are working on. When we are walking in nature, we are drawing in a life force. Much of secular activity dams up feelings. If we cannot give life to what we are doing and we cannot take in life, we become blocked and drained. The world grows stronger and we become weaker, slaves to the vampire that steals away our soul in return for worldly security that can never wholly satisfy us.

What are your thoughts and feelings on reflection?

Is it something you enjoy doing or feel guilty about?

Do you allow yourself time to reflect each day?

Are you aware of how the process works?

Now we have passed through the cycle of reflection we have made sense of everything that has happened to us. We feel a stirring within, a deepening. In that empty place within us we look for peace and all that is borne from love and beauty. This is all that matters. We are emerging from that Dark Night.

Chapter 13

Second Quality of the Wilderness: Contemplation

So far we have reflected on the past, on all the events and cycles which have brought us to where we are now. We have stood back from it long enough in order to fire our arrows towards the future, even if those arrows have not found a lodging place yet. We have withdrawn from the world and opened ourselves to communicate on a soul level with that part of us which cannot always be expressed through matter.

Now, it is time for us to open up further to the wisdom that wants to translate itself to us through our environment and within our immediate surroundings, and to do this we use the medium of contemplation. Even the very word holds clues to its nature: *con-temple - with templum* which literally translated, means 'a place for observations'. There is a sense of standing within a natural observatory, contemplating the heavens, following the trajectories of the planets within our solar system. A sense of, on a deeper level, panning out and taking note of the elements in our lives which drive and compel us to do the things we do. Underneath all the movement is that still place and within that matrix the forces which are omnipresent, omnipotent and omniscient in our life.

Contemplation is neither passive nor inactive. It is a stream of consciousness that can heal, enrich and enlighten us. It can transform us. But primarily, we need to know how to utilize its qualities and realize that it is something which happens quite naturally in childhood, yet too often becomes drowned by all the demands, the *shoulds* and *ifs* of the secular life. In childhood it is often referred to as daydreaming, in adulthood it can be called anything from being lazy to not having your feet on the ground. The world actively discourages contemplation and uses everything within its means to distract us from this natural and sanity saving quality.

As a child, one of my favorite 'daydreams' was sitting at the tea table and looking at the bread, the butter, the jam and thinking about where it had all come from. I would ask myself who had made the bread? And before that, where had the wheat grown? Who had harvested it? Or I would think about the butter; who had milked the cow? And what about the table itself? Where had the wood come from? Where had the tree grown? Who had cut the tree? How many people had it taken to make the table? I imagined all the people in the room, including the cows, hens and trees which had been responsible for everything on the table, and it soon became very crowded the more people I invited in! It also became very interesting. This soon earned me the name of 'daydreamer'. Yet, unknowingly, like so many children, I was in touch with the muse of contemplation. I was in tuition with one of the most well known and sought after philosophers of all time, Sophia the Goddess of wisdom, hence our word, philosophy or *Phil – Sophia*; lover of wisdom.

This form of exercise is very effective in building up a sense of relationship with the world around us when we feel isolated. It quickly identifies a form of interconnectedness that we can relate to on a day to day level.

Today, one of my favorite contemplative tools is an apple. Holding an apple in my hand, I smell it, taste it, feel its firm texture and slowly open myself to its history, its past and future, the complete and endless cycle of its growth, death and regeneration. I think about how it formed from a pip; how the tree grew and passed through the various stages of development, or the seasons until it reached this complete form. I imagine the bud pushing into blossom, and later, underneath the fallen petals, the fruit begins to form and mature, gathering all it needs from its environment, above and below. And then I imagine it falling to the ground, where the various animals and birds enjoy its juicy ripeness, to be passed out and grow again into another tree bearing fruit. It is a miracle. Within this contemplative exercise, I cannot help but see my own growth and development reflected.

So we can understand contemplation is a form of receptivity to whatever object or form we are studying. It is allowing the form to tell us its story and by doing that we find our own. People who have practiced this, especially during the wilderness time, have found it very insightful. And this is why it is especially important to choose a form that we are drawn to; choose it intuitively. It might be a leaf, a shell, a stone, an old vase or a flower. The important thing is that our senses are able to interact with it and that we can hold it.

It is not really important what object we choose, as each form will have its own individual story. In a group, even if all the members were to pick the same object, each person would discover a different insight. For example, I remember carrying out a contemplative exercise where a group of about 30 of us picked a stone to use as our contemplative tool. Some picked stones that had holes in or cracks, and talked about that, others picked smooth stones, large and small stones. Each stone revealed its own story, unique to the individual. I remember being drawn to a smooth round stone that had two adjoining halves of chocolate brown and dove grey. It reminded me of the Chinese Yin and Yang sign; the masculine and feminine and how it was important to harness both these energies in myself. It spoke to me of the dark and light, and how I had come to recognize these tremendous polarities within my own life and how the dark times had opened me more to the light.

In another group exercise, a woman who had suffered the loss of a loved one, had selected the skeleton of a leaf. The fine filigrees which made up the leaf's worn shape, resembled lace and were complete. The woman talked about how, although she had lost a lot of her substance, she was still complete and whole. And even though she was a skeleton, she was still beautiful.

The creative potential of this exercise is illimitable and draws deep on the untapped potential of our consciousness. Moreover, the object's story has a past, present, and future. It may be able to reveal our future for us in ways that very few other things can do. The language of contemplation is very rich in symbolism; therefore it is ageless and ancient. When we are in the wilderness, we are more open to the language of contemplation than at any other time in our lives.

If you want to, you can try this contemplative exercise out on your own. Choose an object that you feel attracted to. It does not matter what it is, even if it is a piece of modern day plastic, it will still have its story.

Let your mind ask questions about it. Allow yourself to wonder about it.

Where did it come from?

Was it a gift from a friend? Did you buy it second hand? Perhaps you found it, or it has been passed down to you? How was it made? Where was it made? Were there people involved in its formation? Can you imagine what they looked like? Were they from this country, or perhaps another? What do you know about that country? What purpose is the object fulfilling in your present life? Is it useful? If so, is it useful to you, someone else, or to nature? Which part of you does it feed? Your body? Your imagination? Your sense of play?

Can you imagine what it's future is? Try to trace where you think that might be. Are you attached to it? How are you attached to it?

Can you now relate this form to yourself, your own life? Does its story speak to you?

Take time out to become aware of the objects around your home. Re-familiarize yourself with ornaments on shelves, dressers, mantelpieces that may have been there so long that you no longer see them. Ask yourself how much they mean to you now. Do you keep them through habit, guilt or do you keep them through sentimentality or genuine love? The objects around us in the home, and these can include paintings, plates, shoes and clothes, are a reflection of us. If they are no longer serving us in some way, then they are cluttering up our life. Do not be afraid to give them away. Giving things away creates room for new conditions and objects to enter our life. And with them they will bring fresh energy and inspiration. Objects should be kept for contemplation, like a beautiful vase or a painting that communicates with us directly through our heart. Historically, when we were more in touch with the earth and our source, we kept objects because they provided protection, power, spiritual guidance and direction. How many of your objects in the home do this for you? Do they give you power or do they drain you as 'clutter' always does?

If you need to become more focused in your life, then give away a few things you no longer need or use. Recycle them. Hoarding possessions can be exhausting and draining, recycling them is freeing, enlivening. Try it and see when you feel things are getting on top of you. This applies to money. The word 'money' comes from the same root word as 'blood' and so therefore needs to circulate. The more you 'give' money away, the more it will return to you. Giving does not mean 'spending', it means giving it away unconditionally to something you believe in; a cause that aids the world in some way. Even if you cannot afford it. No — especially if you cannot afford it! Watch how it returns to you and multiplies?

Ask questions, contemplate, and direction in the form of guidance *will* come.

We have realized our strengths and weaknesses. We have no illusions about what the world can give us or divest us of. The only quality that remains is a ceaseless dedication to what has been revealed to us. We wait with humility for a sense of direction and affirmation.

Chapter 14

Third Quality of Wilderness: Aspiration

At some point the turning back to the past becomes less frequent. There is exhaustion, a giving in, a surrendering, even an admission of complete and utter emptiness and with it arises an inner restlessness which cannot be easily satisfied. Fear may arise as it does with any presentiment of change and movement.

Yet, despite the restlessness, we need to be still, to allow what is within to rise up, to allow new images to emerge. We need to aspire to the highest we can reach, however exhausted we may feel because there is a tendency to be dragged down into depths that will be difficult to emerge from. Even in the depths we need a vision, a goal. At the bottom of a well we can see the stars. We may not reach them, but visualization of them will bring the stars nearer to ourselves. As above, so below. The only barrier between the stars and us is the personality.

We also need to remind ourselves that although the personality is uncomfortable, the soul is no longer asleep, it is awake. We have to feed our soul. It is waiting and hungry for real sustenance. Soul language is different to personality language. Competition, self-expression and self-esteem along with all the trappings of the ego mean very little to it. It knows of pain and joy and these are different to personality pain which hungers for gratification that is always fleeting. The soul understands the pain of yearning for its spiritual home and union with Divine. It understands restlessness. And although it possesses vast reservoirs of patience and understanding, it is relentless in its quest back to its source — long outliving the present body and personality. Shaped from the stars, it travels with us through eternity, all the time growing in strength and awareness, breaking time and time through the constraints of the personality in an explosion of exquisite color and beauty. Once awake, it can never return to sleep. As it gathers in strength and finds its true direction, we learn to trust it and it becomes our teacher, comrade and friend.

But, right now, it wants food of the spiritual kind and it will not give us any rest until it finds it. The soul's persistence in leading us where we need to go, is the 'love that will not let us go' or so finely illustrated in Francis Thompson's classical poem *The Hound of Heaven*, where that force the protagonist or poet runs away from, is the love that he seeks.

This need for spiritual nourishment, when understood, is not just a matter of devouring endless self-help books on spiritual development, or signing up for a plethora of workshops which, although very tempting, can be just another form of escapism. It is more about using what is available to us and trusting our intuition. It may be simply making use of what our environment holds for us, rather than what we feel it lacks! If we are open and receptive to our environment, it will be open and receptive towards us. Our working and living environment provides an ideal form of mirroring which range from abandoned talents to ones we may be too afraid to realize for fear of being different, standing out or even daring to shine!

During any wilderness experience, as the desert fathers found, it is easier to communicate with nature than people, unless they are the 'right kind', namely sensitive to our soul needs! Whatever the reasons, the 'right people' seem in very short supply during the wilderness time! They either speak a language we appear to have lost the ability to use or are genuinely unavailable. It is as if we are *invisible* — and maybe we are!

If we do not have a garden, our link with nature may be through a park, a small wood, a nearby lake, the canal or, if we are lucky, the sea. Even in the most built up places, I have often discovered, there are 'boltholes' to the modern day wilderness. If you are disabled in some way so that you cannot physically go out or make contact with the natural environment, it may be only available through the window. Whatever the disability, there is always the opportunity. So even if the view onto the countryside is unavailable, it is an opportunity to discover nature through meditation or simple visualization exercises. The whole wilderness experience invites us to utilize the power of our inner senses rather than our outer ones. Health shops and most book stores abound with meditation exercises on tape with enhancement through sound and music; many of which are interwoven with the sounds of nature.

Remember, you do not have to reach out to your environment, but rather through cultivating an inner stillness, your environment will unfold around and within you, strand by strand.

It is helpful to know what to look for and how: Which way is the wind blowing? Are the clouds high, or low? Are they stretched out like feathers or clumped together like cauliflowers. What does the air smell of? Can you smell fragrance, damp leaves, blossom or the slightly chill scent of the fall? Do these scents evoke memories from the past?

Find something beautiful in your day, on your walk; perhaps a rainbow through rain drops, or the way the sun caches the dew on the grass or a spider's web; the pellucid note of a bird. Feed the soul!

Although we may appear invisible to people, nature does see us and acknowledge us. Aware of our emptiness, she longs to fill it like the Great Mother she is. Leaves or blossoms fall onto our hair, acorns tap our shoes, our shoulders. Feathers brush our cheek. A butterfly settles on the tree or flower we are contemplating or dances in front of us. Squirrels leap before us, chattering wildly, chasing each other. Roots and twigs playfully trip us up. It is as if nature is using every means available to grab our attention. She not only acknowledges us, she welcomes us as we gradually feel ourselves relaxing and surrendering to her presence. Where, before, we might have felt indifferent to nature, even a stranger, now we are no longer outsiders, we very much belong. Instead, the secular world has become the outsider. We may even enter the world of synchronicity where symbols and totems that hold significance for us come to greet us time and time again. For example, one of my personal symbols is the dragonfly. Always, when I am passing through a challenging experience or perhaps going somewhere that is unfamiliar, a dragonfly will buzz me. They appear in the most unlikely places, in railway stations, in airports, darting above me in busy towns as well as the more obvious places. One October, I even had a beautiful hawker settle to die on my back doorstep. I was privi- leged to gaze into the beautiful turquoise prisms of its eyes and enjoy its iridescent colors before it died. I still have that hawker on my bookshelf, although the color has long left its body and wings. When dragonflies are not in season, they continue to visit me in cards from friends and even communications from a stranger who knew nothing about my passion for dragonflies. Guided by their intuition, a part of their soul knows how to communicate with mine.

I had a friend who worked in a bank and she once told me how she finds feathers everywhere as her symbol, again in unlikely places, like department stores, left for her on chairs, in lifts, in filing cabinets. She said that someone once told her that when she found a feather, it meant an angel had passed that way. I always think of that when I see feathers now and conclude there must be a lot of angels passing backwards and forwards!

Another friend often paints wolves or finds symbols of them when she needs confirmation. She is a teacher and so is the wolf the teacher in the medicine wheel. As symbols and totems come to us, we do not have to go looking for them. They follow us around as if they were attached to us – and they probably are, since everything in the world is inter-related! Some people's symbols are white doves, others butterflies, kingfishers or certain flowers or trees. Symbols and totems when recognized lift us out of the mundane. They help us to aspire. We do not have to be psychic to have them, we just need to have our eyes open and be willing to expand and change.

Do you have a symbol that is important to you?

The breakthrough has been made. Nature has become our refuge; we accept what she has been endeavoring to give us all along. Nature does not judge us as we judge ourselves or think others do. She not only accepts our emptiness, but she embraces it.

Gradually we begin to see through her eyes – or rather realize our own natural vision. We communicate to the soul through its senses. We play beautiful music. We burn incense. We read books that elevate the mind and communicate directly to our spirit. And even if we choose not to do this, we find our own way. We aspire, reach upwards to the spiritual vistas which both fill us with yearning and yet are the only thing that can sate that same yearning.

The worst thing we can do is to run back into the world; fill our lives with activity and turn our backs on our soul. Invariably this backfires and we suffer a setback of some kind or our carefully constructed plans hit the wall. The more we struggle against this experience, the more the world fights back. And it should never be forgotten that however great our intentions, our soul is *always* stronger than our mind, our ego, our body.

The soul will not let us go. It will wear us down night after wakeful night, day after day until in desperation we turn and look at it and listen to its needs.

Completion of the Cycle

Having passed through the *Stripping* to become embedded in the *Long Wait* we have been tested further by entering the *Wilderness*. Now, having integrated our past experience we have freed ourselves from its power over us. Yet – we carry the seeds of the new within us to begin another cycle. The wisdom we have gained through the three-fold process of reflection, contemplation and aspiration we can now use in the world. We have honed our life experience into food and insight we can share with others on the journey. We have realized a complete map of consciousness within us, so that we not only know where we are in our inner, creative process, but also to bring vision to those who may not have been able to harness their insight into working tools for themselves and others.

Conclusion

My purpose of writing this work was to invite the reader or teacher into the natural environment that, as human beings we are an integral part of. Nature is not external to our everyday experience. The buildings we live in have materials harnessed from the natural environment whether it is stone, rock, steel or cement. The vehicles of transport we use to move around in are created from raw energies of the earth which, like the crystals we cherish, have been buried for millions of years.

The late Norwegian philosopher, Arne Naess, believed that until we can as a race develop a sense of deep ecology, which is an intimate sense of union with nature, we cannot make that final step to working with nature, rather than working against and upon the natural environment.

Today our conversation revolves around 'saving the planet' which is not entirely true. The planet has been through mass extinctions before where conditions have not been possible to harbor such a prolific sense of life forms as we have known in our own lifetime. And, indeed, the lifetime of the generations which preceded us. In reality it is ourselves we are wanting to save because we cannot live on the earth without each and every other life form besides ourselves. Historically, we have witnessed the extinction of civilizations like those on Easter Island and the Maya culture because of overpopulation and deforestation and loss of habitat for the animals. This work's small part in this process illustrates a cyclical template that plays itself out again and again in the natural world. Furthermore, this translates into our own personal lives where we exist within a biosphere largely of our own making. Bringing consciousness to this process, opens up possibilities of deep connection with life and each other. I do believe that our collective longing is for meaning, purpose and value in our lives which cannot be found in a material world that exiles nature as our greatest teacher. The natural environment, whether it be in the form of the waves on the beach, or the wind in the trees or the awesome flight of migrating birds, speaks to us again and again, calling us back to that sense of unity which the North American Indian knew, as did our shamanic ancestors of old. Connection brings us in touch with presence, with God, with spirituality...

Appendix

About six months into beginning this book, I had one of those amazingly lucid dreams when it seemed as if all the senses you have and do not know you have, were turned on. I was aware of this vast tree presence of great love and wisdom speaking through the fibers of the dream. When I awoke, I knew I had to write down the dream and try and coax the words to life on paper. Although I cannot write the words exactly as they came, I hope you can see beyond the words to something more....

I DREAMED GOD WAS A TREE

I dreamed I went to heaven in search of that which shaped and set me into being.....

I found myself at the foot of a great tree. Its mighty trunk was whorled and woven with sunshine. And the star sculpted branches reaching up to forever, seemed vast enough to cradle the light years themselves.

I became small within myself and bowed beneath such a sight. Each shimmering leaf was veined with a beauty that was exquisite. The fruits were softly rounded suns which made my whole being glow with warmth and, overcome with awe, I closed my eyes. The perfumed breeze which wafted about me was resonant with silvery voices.

I knew even before I opened my eyes that the shining trees which circled the Great Tree were the archangels of heaven. Chanting like some majestic choir, I experienced the sound of it

167

flowing into me, assuaging the aching hungry places within me.

I became still within myself as the chanting ebbed away. Out of this grew a mighty silence that made my heart quicken. No – it was as if the quickening were in the depths of my soul.

'Why have you come?' the Great Tree spoke.

There was the mountain in the timbre of the voice, yet the softness of falling dew too.

The child within me replied: 'I wanted to meet the One who made me.'

'And?'

'Are – you the One?'

The silence was enough; for it seemed to contain so much.

'Yes,' the Great Tree spoke, 'You are my fruit.'

My words rushed out clumsily. 'I thought — I mean — I thought you would be remote... like cloud stuff or angel wings. But — you're solid.'

'Touch me,' the Great Tree invited. 'Go on....'

A heat pulsed in me as the wood swelled and breathed beneath my fingers. Underneath I felt the patience of the earth and the vastness of a force which was illimitable. And the heat flowed through me in warm honeyed waves, infusing me with a sweetness that could be nothing other than pure love.

'Am I remote?' the Great Tree asked?

'No – that is impossible,' I heard myself say. 'You are full of light and love!'

A tremor ran through the tree and the leaves quivered so that prisms of light scattered in jewels across the soft green woodland floor.

'I am everything you are,' spoke the Great Tree.' And all that you can ever be.... I am all around you. My roots run forever beneath you, and my branches uphold the deep blue of the sky.'

The tree's voice was mighty, although it never once lost its healing depths. Its words seem to fall about me in gentle hues as if they contained the colors of the rainbow as well as the music of an invisible orchestra.

'... I am in your world too,' the tree continued.

And I didn't know if the sadness I experienced just then was the Great Tree's or my own. 'I know – but we have cut you down and turned you into money and paper we cover with untruths.' I replied. 'There are too few artists who can inscribe the paper which is your body with a beauty parallel with your own.'

Another tremble ran through the Great Tree and through all the other trees who were the Archangels. 'You cut me down and destroy me because you do not know me. But I tell you that you want me so much that you are blind to your wanting. I surrender to your chisel, your nails and steel blades and still you do not see me. And because you do not know me, you fear me.'

Again the Great Tree trembled. I knew that it was not fear that caused it to tremble, but a love deeper than I could imagine which was older than the earth, time even.

'When you destroy me, cut me down, burn me – this is what you do also to yourself,' the tree spoke again.' For I am the air you breathe and the shade which protects you from a light and heat that is sometimes too bright to bear.'

The Great Tree really was speaking in colors, for a rainbow arched out across the trees; eddying out and out to break off and become miniature pools of color. And each color held a fragrance which seemed to assuage a hunger that I had barely known existed in my soul.

'... I am also the food that sustains you. And the deep wisdom that rises up in a fountain to flow like honey through your soul when you, in your grief and loneliness, reach out and open yourself to me.'

The tree seemed to smile and it was a dancing deep within me.

But the adult within me hung its head in shame. 'I am sorry – for what we have done.'

'Do not pity me,' the tree spoke in deeper tones. 'Pity

yourselves in your unknowing.... I am eternal. I straddle the depths of time and space to birth new stars. With my breath I set the spiral and shimmering of new galaxies in motion. With my deep compassion for all that has not been created and has no voice I dance you into being. And your own world is a precious jewel that cannot be destroyed..... You can only destroy yourselves so that you return to the soundless deep which ever craves for birth.'

In the silence that followed, the colors had merged to become a brightness that was pure light, and it was as if the Great Tree had become transparent so that I could see the form inside. Before me was a most beautiful angelic being, prismatic and shimmering? But the eyes were still and somehow vast. They were the eyes of Christ, of Buddha, Kuan Yin, Koot Humi, and all the Great Masters that had ever walked the earth. And yet it was the eyes of every young child and animal I had looked at with kindness and compassion. Eyes which were ancient and new, wise and innocent. Eyes that were the source of life. And as I gazed out across the other trees, I was able to see their proud and beautiful forms in the wood. There all around me like great tribal chieftains whose features were honed from earth and wood and leaf.

'Can't you stop us destroying ourselves?' I asked.

The tree crooned deep within itself and a hush fell upon the trees.

'No,' the tree spoke at length. 'But ... you can.'

'I ? But I am so small... There's so little I can do.'

I felt the tree smiled even though its voice remained the same.

'That is because you think in terms of limitation – because you forget who you are and where you have come from... When you truly understand that you are part of creation, then you give up your isolation. By doing this you connect with me and bloom and become my fruit, then your power is limitless. You must also remember that even though the seed may feel cut off from its source, it holds everything it needs within it.... I too was a seed once... Yes, I began as you – one tiny dream in the deep mystery of being with the awareness that I had access to something far greater then myself, a source that was illimitable... I struggled for light as you have done. I felt the fear of the unknown as my buds swelled and burst open, for I felt naked and exposed. But then, I experienced my first blossoming and I was infused with the incense of love and beauty.... Ah – I inhaled the quiet shining of the stars.'

It was as if the Great Tree were talking in pictures, for all it had expressed flowed into my mind and every nerve and sense of my being had become attuned to what was being described, until I felt it as my own. I too experienced the lonely vigil of the stars, and yet their terrifying beauty too. I too inhaled the solidity of the great rocks and felt the patient aspiration of the mountain.

The tree sighed and a shadow fell across its trunk as if some of the light had died. 'But then the blossom fell and I experienced a deep sense of loss and abandonment – as if I had fallen from Grace.'

The tree's experience was my own. I had known what it was to feel a sense of union with another, only to have it slip mysteriously away, leaving me stranded in the shadows, naked but for my helplessness.

The light surged forward again, thrusting back the shadow. 'But then the growth came,' the Great Tree's voice was labored. 'And when it came it was slow and painful. It was growth into the unknown. I was afraid as the young bird taking its first flight into the great void. Blinded as the caterpillar in its cocoon, suffocated as the dragonfly larvae at the bottom of the muddy pond, yet knowing that to give up was to die.' The vision enveloped me so that I was caught up in its shape, color and form. I was sent spiraling out across the star systems until I finally awoke on my own planet and within the body where my spirit resided.

I dreamed that I went to heaven to see that which shaped me and found that God was a tree.

References

Introduction

Burnett, Francis, *The Secret Garden*, Candlewick, 2008

Alighieri,Dante, *The Divine Comedy*, Oxford Paperback,1998

Diamond, Jared, *Collapse, How Societies Choose to Fail or Survive*, Penguin,2005

Eliot, T.S, *Four Quartets*, Faber and Faber, 1984

Yeats, *The Second Coming*,
 http://www.potw.org/archive/potw351.html

Chapter 1: Nature as Mirror

Grut, Jenny, Linden, Sonja, *The Healing Fields*, Frances Lincoln Publishers Ltd, 2002

Hill, Butterfly,Julia, *The legacy of Luna*, Harper,Collins, 2000

Yalom, D, Irvin, *Staring at the Sun, Overcoming the Dread of Death*, Piatakus, 2008

Chapter 2: Using the Mirror

Sears, William, *God Loves Laughter*, George Ronald; New impression edition (Aug 1968)

Buber, Martin, *I and Thou*, Continuum International Publishing Group Ltd, 2004

Chapter 3: The Tree as Model

Assagioli, Roberto, *Psychosynthesis*, HarperCollins, 1993

Blyton, Enid, *The Faraway Tree*, Egmont Books, 2007

Bortoft, Henri, *The Wholeness of Nature: Goethe's Way of Science*, Floris books, 1996

Suzuki and Grady, *Tree, A Life Story*, Greystone Books, Vancouver, 2004

http://www.noblood.org/did-you-know/2823-chlorophyl-instead-blood.html

Chapter 6: Late Spring: Blossoming

Edwards, Betty, *Drawing on the Artist Within*, HarperCollins, 1995

Chapter 8: Late Summer: Harvest

Selection of books by Henry Thomas Hamblin available from www.thehamblintrust.org.uk

Chapter 10: Winter

Eliot, T.S, *Four Quartets: East Coker*, Faber paperbacks, 1979

Hillman, James, *The Soul's Code*, Bantam Books 1997

Lozoff, Bo, *We're All Doing Time*, Human Kindness Foundation, 1998

Wilber, Ken, *A Theory of Everything*, Gateway, 2001

Chapter 14: Aspiration

Thompson, Francis, *The Hound of Heaven and other Poems*, Branden Publishing Co, U.S. 2003

B O O K S

O is a symbol of the world, of oneness and unity. In different cultures it also means the "eye," symbolizing knowledge and insight. We aim to publish books that are accessible, constructive and that challenge accepted opinion, both that of academia and the "moral majority."

Our books are available in all good English language bookstores worldwide. If you don't see the book on the shelves ask the bookstore to order it for you, quoting the ISBN number and title. Alternatively you can order online (all major online retail sites carry our titles) or contact the distributor in the relevant country, listed on the copyright page.

See our website **www.o-books.net** for a full list of over 500 titles, growing by 100 a year.

And tune in to myspiritradio.com for our book review radio show, hosted by June-Elleni Laine, where you can listen to the authors discussing their books.

MySpiritRadio